W9-AZM-176

More Urgent Than Usual

The Final Homilies
of Mark Hollenhorst

Edited by
William C. Graham

A Liturgical Press Book

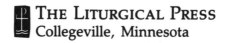

THE LITURGICAL PRESS
Collegeville, Minnesota

Cover design by David Manahan, O.S.B.
Cover photo by Thomas Ferrian.

Photo on page viii reproduced with permission of the Duluth-News Tribune.

1   2   3   4   5   6   7   8

Library of Congress Cataloging-in-Publication Data

Hollenhorst, Mark, d. 1993.
    More urgent than usual : the final homilies of Mark Hollenhorst / edited by
  William C. Graham.
        p.   cm.
    ISBN 0-8146-2356-5
    1. Church year sermons.   2. Hollenhorst, Mark, d. 1993—Sermons.
  3. Death—Religious aspects—Catholic Church—Sermons.   4. Sermons,
  English.   I. Graham, William C., 1950-   .   II. Title.
  BX1756.H65M67   1995
  252'.02—dc20   95-13675
                                                                    CIP

The longer we live,
the closer we all get to our deaths.
So I guess my situation isn't really much different
from anybody else's.
It's just a little more imminent to me.
Consequently, today's Gospel also seems to be
a little more urgent than usual.

Mark Hollenhorst
July 24, 1993

If the Lord's passion is a sham, so is my being in chains.
As it is, however, I have given myself up completely
to death, fire, sword and wild beasts.
For the simple reason that near the sword
means near to God.
But, it must all be in the name of Jesus Christ.
To share in his passion, I go through everything.
For he who became the perfect man gives me strength.
Come fire, cross, battling with wild beasts,
wrenching of bones, mangling of limbs,
crushing of my whole body, cruel tortures of any kind
—only let me get to God.
If suffer I must, I shall be emancipated by Jesus Christ;
and, united to him, I shall rise to freedom!

Ignatius of Antioch

To
Robert and Alice Hollenhorst
who loved Mark into life,
and to the priests and people
of the Diocese of Duluth
who nurtured and sustained him,
and to his friends and associates
at St. John's Parish in Grand Marais
and Holy Rosary Parish in Grand Portage
who walked with him the final miles.

Contents

The Paschal Mystery

Ashes, Lent, and Easter

Seeds of the Kingdom

More Urgent Than Usual

Afterword

Foreword

Mark Hollenhorst was unconventional and even eccentric in most areas of his life. When we were seminarians and young priests, I would often tell him that when we grew old and people would comment on how eccentric he had become, I would be quick to assert that his ways were not a product of advanced age, but had been remarkable even in his youth. Dead at forty-three years of age, he will not now grow old with us, but his memory will quicken us in faith.

Mark was unconventional in his approach to school. He was bright enough to do very well, with time left over for bridge, pinochle, and television. His approach to interior decoration was a ready admission that he was hardly a "neat freak." And, when last I consulted my *Funk and Wagnall's* for the definition of "peripatetic," I found there an eight-by-ten glossy picture of his smiling face. He would travel hours and miles in circuitous routes for the sheer pleasure of movement and scenery.

He was a true fan of both popular and high culture. Like Pope Paul VI, Mark understood that the sacred was the secular as seen in the light of God's plan. His tastes were therefore eclectic, ranging from *Sesame Street* to Bruckner.

Clearly, Wisdom found her home in Mark's heart: "passing into holy souls from age to age, / she produces friends of God and prophets" (Wis 7:27). Wisdom's indwelling was the most remarkable of all Mark's traits, yielding a profound holiness. This holiness had its roots in his strong family, was nourished in study and prayer, particularly under and with the Benedictines at our beloved St. John's in Collegeville, and reached an edifying summit in his pastorate at St. John's Parish in Grand Marais, Minnesota, on the chilly and awe-inspiring shores of Lake Superior. I took Mark's place there for a weekend in August, 1993, and was moved by the transformation of a worshiping community walking with their pastor and friend through the final stages of illness, preparing with steady grace to see the face of God. His death on the Feast of St. John was not a coincidence, but God's gift of one beloved disciple as guide to another on the last steps of earthly pilgrimage.

This holy man who lived with us and challenged us to be kind in dealing with one another and insightful in seeking God taught us not to fear death, but to embrace life.

It is clear that we, the Church, have an obligation to announce holiness when it is found in our midst. In this way, we proclaim God's grace active in our world. During his final summer, I asked him for permission to edit his homilies. It will be clear to the reader that Mark's last trip through the Lectionary is a guide through the liturgical year, as well as a companion to us as we endure the vicissitudes of life. In homely moments, he saw and loved God. This wise guide will help the reader to see and to pray.

Like many an inspired preacher, Mark made use of any number of sources. Most often they were given credit in the course of his homily. I have attempted to secure permission for the use of quotes whenever possible. Should there be any unauthorized use of another's work, or, worse, an unattributed use, please contact me with the proper information, and any future printing will be amended.

Together, Mark and I decided that royalties from the sale of this book would be used to establish a fund for the continuing education of the clergy in the Diocese of Duluth. Royalties will be invested until the year 2025, when Mark might have retired. At that time, the Bishop of the Diocese and his associates can make a gift of education to someone who will announce the Good News to a new generation. Readers who wish to make a tax deductible gift to be added to this fund may send a check to The Mark Hollenhorst Fund at the Pastoral Center for the Diocese of Duluth, 2830 East Fourth Street, Duluth, Minnesota 55812.

Please savor this book one homily at a time during the appointed seasons or in those moments you feel moved to prayerfulness. Mark's great and homely gift for seeking God in each day's trials and delights is sure to provide ready access to grace. With the help of his prayers, may we all meet one day in the fullness of God's good peace.

William C. Graham
Harlem, on Manhattan's Upper East Side
18 March 1994
Friday of the Fourth Week of Lent
on the Memorial of Cyril of Jerusalem

Acknowledgments

I am grateful to all who have contributed to getting this work into print.

Mark's parents, Dr. Robert and Mrs. Alice Hollenhorst, have been not just supportive, but eager to assist in collecting, critiquing, encouraging, and even translating hand written or typed texts into computer files. Mark's sister Kathy Stassen has also been helpful.

Fr. Michael Naughton, O.S.B., of The Liturgical Press, remembered Mark from our student days, and was both kind and encouraging. I am very grateful to him.

Sr. Patrice Werner, O.P., as academic dean and president-designate of Caldwell College in Caldwell, New Jersey, provided student assistance to me in the preparation of this manuscript. To her, and to Steve Auxter and Joe Mathesius, able typists, I am also grateful.

The Beginning of the End

There is cause for rejoicing here.
You may for a time have to suffer
the distress of many trials;
but this is so that your faith,
which is more precious
than the passing splendor of fire-tried gold,
may by its genuineness
lead to praise, glory, and honor
when the Lord Jesus Christ appears.
Although you have never seen him,
you love him,
and without seeing you now believe in him,
and rejoice with inexpressible joy
touched with glory
because you are achieving faith's goal,
your salvation.

1 Peter 1:6-9

I Am Going to Leave this World a Happy Man

At Easter two years ago, I played for you one of my favorite pieces of music: the last three exciting minutes of Bruckner's Fourth Symphony, one of the greatest passages in all of music. You may remember that, at the time, I told you that Bruckner described it as the sun rising gloriously over the majestic mountains. Advent is a time to look forward to that same kind of light: the light of Jesus our Savior that shines in our world during the Christmas season.

I had the wonderful opportunity, a week ago Friday, to hear the Minnesota Orchestra play Bruckner's Fourth Symphony in its entirety at Orchestra Hall. The performance was spectacular, to say the least.

I listened with mixed emotions though. As the music progressed toward the powerful conclusion, the excitement kept mounting. But I also had a growing sadness that it would all soon be over. I wanted it to last forever. So the closer it got to the end, the more I appreciated each individual note. When it was over, there was great sadness in me; I did not want to leave; I wanted to hear it all over again. But I left the concert a richer person, and grateful to God for giving me such a wonderful experience.

My life has been like that concert the last couple of weeks. I've been thinking about life and death a lot lately because my cancer has come back. And I know now that I am a lot closer to my death than I am to my birth. I found out this week that one of my ribs is disintegrating. It sounds worse than it feels. It doesn't hurt much. Every once in a while, if I strain it the wrong way, it feels kind of like sore muscles after a heavy work-out.

When I got the news, my first response was: "Doc, you gotta be ribbin' me!" But it was strikingly easy for me to take. I was actually more distressed by the Vikings' loss to the Lions last week.

I go back next week to find out what happens next, and what kind of treatment I need. Hopefully, God will give me many more good years of life, but I'm ready for whatever comes.

Life on earth is a wonderful gift to us from God. It's like listening to that Bruckner Symphony—full of beauty, tension, struggle, joy, sorrow, hope, and, at times, profound peace. I wish life could go on forever, but I know it is drawing to a close. There is a sadness in that, but consequently, every breath becomes richer and every moment is appreciated all the more. And when it comes time to die, I know that I am going to leave this world a happy man, grateful to God for having given me the experience.

We are all in the same boat, really; some of us just have a better indication of the time frame. Today's Gospel offers us a great hope in the face of our transient and all too brief existence on earth. It says that we have something to look forward to at the end of our lives. Something as glorious as the end of Bruckner's Fourth Symphony awaits us all. We will see Christ face-to-face and we will live with him forever. I believe this Gospel, and that is why I have very little distress about my condition. I am ready to take whatever comes, because I know that something wonderful lies just beyond it.

I have accepted my condition and actually look on my cancer as a gift to me from God to help teach me more about the beauty of life.

I look at it this way: if it is true that the more my cancer grows, the closer I get to death, and if the Gospel is also true in saying that we will see the glory of Christ face-to-face after our life on earth ends, then, to me, it appears that my cancer is the way through which I will get to God.

Delivered at the Church of St. John in Grand Marais on the First Sunday of Advent December 1, 1991

Attention Focused on the Goal
Gives Me Hope to Endure

When I sat down a few days ago, on Thursday morning, to read the scriptures for today's Mass, and started to think about this homily, I was grateful for Paul's letter to the Philippians. In fact, it touched me so deeply that I began to cry. If I tried for a million years to tell you how I feel about having terminal cancer, I could never say it any better than by just repeating these words of St. Paul.

One of the phrases that caught my eye was this: "I wish to know Christ and the power flowing from his resurrection!"

That is what this season is all about. We suffer and die symbolically in little ways during Lent so that we can celebrate Easter, when it comes, with a renewed spirit of faith. Through the Easter celebration, we get a little taste of heaven and it helps us to trust in the resurrection. It helps us to really accept what God tells the Israelites in the first reading: "God has the power to make all things new!"

For a person in my situation, that gives me a great deal of comfort and hope, because it helps me to believe that God has at least one of two fantastic things in store for me. Either he will cure me in this life, or, after my death, he will raise me up on the last day so that I can experience a total Easter of eternal joy! Either way, it surely looks like a bright future for me.

A second phrase from Paul's letter that struck me is this: "Likewise, I wish to know how to share in Christ's sufferings being formed into the pattern of his death!"

Cancer is a very interesting disease, and it does interesting things to people's emotions. What I am going to say now is a generalization, and it is not always true. I think there is some merit in saying it anyway. People who have someone they love with cancer tend to think of it as a terrible disease because it causes suffering and it is going to take their loved one away. Last night, on TV, I saw an advertisement from a cancer clinic in which Marlo Thomas called cancer a "big bully." I think that is the general picture that most people without cancer have.

People with cancer, on the other hand, react a little differently. If you look at us, generally you see seemingly reasonably happy people. We all have suffering in life; nobody can escape it. Cancer is just one of many forms of human suffering. We learn to live with it fairly easily, and can even appreciate it. I've said before, and I've heard from many others, that my cancer is a gift to me from God. I'd certainly like to be healed from it, but that is not essential for my happiness because I know that Christ is with me in my need.

When I suffer, it gives me the chance to identify with Christ's sufferings and reflect on how much he had to endure for my salvation. It makes me love him all the more. Sometimes I sit in front of the crucifix and marvel at Christ's passion and death, and find myself overcome by a state of ecstasy. I feel like I am in total union with him.

How many of you've seen the movie *Prince of Tides*? I love the final scene in which Nick Nolte is driving across the high bridge in Charleston as he reflects on the special woman-psychiatrist in his life who liberated him from the demons that haunted him from the past and imprisoned his present. She cured him and gave him the freedom to live again. As he reaches the crest of the bridge, he feels a spontaneous surge of love welling up inside, and he blurts out her name from the depths of his heart: "Lowenstein! Lowenstein!"

I have a love like that in my life, too! Sometimes, when I am driving along in my car, I find myself speaking the name out loud: "Jesus Christ! Jesus Christ!" I look at this cross, and I see the man who willingly died for me out of love. And I want to return the favor. A feeling of gratitude overwhelms me when I think that he suffered all of this for me. His death has liberated me from my sins, and I am free to live again, because of his sacrifice.

I was happy to see that Anthony Hopkins received the Academy Award for best actor this year. It's long overdue. He gives one spectacular performance after another. He was superb as Captain Bligh in *Mutiny on the Bounty,* and as Richard Lionheart in *The Lion in Winter*. His best performance, though, was about ten years back in a TV miniseries called *Peter and Paul*. He gave a sense of how close he was to Jesus Christ. In the final scene, just before the ax comes down to behead him, he says simply one word: "Jesus!" It is apparent that, to St. Paul, Jesus is not someone who is up there or over in the tabernacle. Jesus is right inside us, a close and personal friend who shares every joy and sorrow of our lives.

I want to be like St. Paul, to feel Christ's presence inside. Sometimes I do. But I want to be able to utter the same words that St. Paul did when he once wrote, "It is not I who suffer; it is Christ who suffers in me."

A third phrase that sprang out at me from today's epistle is this: "My entire attention is on the finish line as I run toward the prize to which God calls me, life on high in Jesus Christ."

It is interesting to observe the way people react to cancer. Some talk about winning or losing the fight with cancer. I am not aware of any contest. One takes what is available, does what seems best, and is grateful for the gifts the doctors can give. I have always maintained that winning is a silly illusion, and I am happy to see that a great new sports movie, *White Men Can't Jump,* agrees with me in which a star basketball player is sorely defeated, and his girl friend tries to console him by insisting that winning and losing are all part of the same organic globule.

The only real struggle is a spiritual one, to align our wills with God's. This is the same struggle that Jesus went through in the garden of Gethsemane. The physical outcome will take care of itself because God is in control and knows what's best for us before we even ask.

Like St. Paul, I have my vision set on that final goal too. The only problem is that I cannot see the finish line ahead of me. I do not know if I have six months or six years left in this world. I hope the doctors at the Mayo Clinic can give me some indication when I go there for tests after Easter.

Right now, it is difficult for me to make any plans or commitments. The parish council talks about making a three-year plan for the parish. That is great, but I really do not know if I'll be around that long. I would like to go to Europe in six weeks—I've already bought my airline ticket—but I have no idea how I will feel at that time. Maybe I will have to junk the whole thing before then.

If the doctors could tell me, "Mark, you're going to start getting really sick on February 10, 1993!" Or, "You will die at eight o'clock in the morning on October 1, 1995!"; then I could see the finish line and know what to focus my attention on in my life.

As it is, I feel kind of like I did when I back-packed in the mountains of New Mexico a few years back. We had a mountain to climb.

We would look ahead on the path and see a ridge and think, "Great! There's the top. We've almost made it." We would struggle to get to the top of the ridge and, when we made it, to our horror, we would see another ridge ahead of us with another five hundred feet of altitude to knock off. We all knew what was beyond that one—another ridge to climb, and another, and another.

Like St. Paul, I have confidence in the fact that the finish line is out there. Like the mountain trip, I know that there is still a lot of beauty to go through before I get there. But I still keep my attention focused on that goal line because it gives me the hope I need to endure. As Paul's fourth phrase says, "Thus do I hope that I may arrive at the resurrection from the dead!" And that hope keeps me going too.

We who are about to die tend to worry a little bit about what the last judgment is going to be like. Am I going to be good enough to get to heaven? Well, only God is holy and without sin.

Today's Gospel sets my heart at ease. It is great to read these stories of God's forgiveness. Jesus says, "Woman, where did they all disappear to? Is there no one left to condemn you? Nor do I condemn you. You may go. But, from now on, avoid this sin!"

On the last day, it is going to be one-on-one in the same way. And I am glad it is Jesus to whom I must answer. He seems very compassionate and forgiving. I suspect he will offer me a seat at the kitchen table, pour me a glass of water, and we'll just sit there and talk about the old times. He will thank me for the good moments, forgive me for the bad, and invite me to share new life and friendship with him.

Of course, we need not wait until the last days for an experience like that. The sacrament of reconciliation is available any time.

This week, I celebrated the sacrament with another priest, and it is a great feeling. I would encourage all of you to do the same in the next couple of weeks. It is a great way to prepare for Easter and to share in Christ and the power flowing from his resurrection. It is the best way I know of coming back to him with all our hearts.

Delivered at the Church of St. John in Grand Marais on the Fifth Sunday of Lent April 5, 1992

God Has One of Two Fantastic Things in Store for Me

The snow is melting. The birds have returned. The trees are coming back to life. Spring is here, and it sets my heart to dancing. This is the time of year that I love to get out and hike the trails, climb the bluffs to spectacular views, sit beside a powerful waterfall, take in its fascinating patterns of running water and absorb its beautiful sounds. I get a little taste of heaven, and it gives me the encouragement to believe even more!

God, who has crafted this beautiful world, loves it even more than we do. He even loves us more than we love ourselves. He sent Christ into this world to redeem us. In this Easter season, we celebrate Christ's death and resurrection. Spring is a gift to us from God to remind us that he had the power to bring a dead world back to life.

Through our celebration of Easter, we get a little taste of heaven, and that sweet taste helps us to trust in the resurrection.

For a person in my situation, with untreatable thyroid cancer, that taste gives me a great deal of comfort and hope, for it helps me to believe that God has at least one of two fantastic things in store for me: either he will cure me in this life; or, after my death, he will raise me up on the last day, so I may experience a total Easter of eternal joy! Either way, it surely looks like a bright future.

Faith makes such a resurrection possible for each one of us both in our present lives and in the life to come. Pray for the faith and share in God's new life. Amen. Alleluia!

Delivered at the Church of St. John in Grand Marais on Easter Sunday April 19, 1992

More Than a Tour Guide!

One of the really great delights of my trip to Europe was my traveling companion, Fr. Whitney Evans of Duluth. He had been to Europe three times previous to this trip and, for me, he was a perfect tour guide. I put my total trust in him and was never disappointed.

In addition to knowing how to get around on public transportation, where to go, what to see, and which hotels to stay in each night, he was also very knowledgeable about the culture and history of Europe. He is a professor of history at the College of St. Scholastica in Duluth, and his presence on the trip was like carrying an encyclopedia wherever we went, without the hassle of the extra load. He was an instant source of excellent information. He told me that if I paid the one thousand dollar tuition fee, I could get three college credits in history. Considering the cost of a Coke in Paris, that price doesn't seem to be too exorbitant.

Each one of us has a great friend like that on our trip through life—*Jesus Christ, our Lord and Redeemer.* Like Father Whitney, he is a master of this world that we are all traveling through; he knows all the ins and outs. He knows what is best for us in this life, and he is loaded with information and knowledge about the real values of human existence. After all, as last week's first reading reminded us, he was around here since the beginning of time when God created the world. Even more than that, he willingly came to earth as a human being like us, and lived a quality life before us. So he really knows what he's talking about.

He has the answer to every question we could ever hope to ask. As he said himself, "I am the way, the truth, and the life. I am the Word of God and the light of the world!"

It seems to me that for us to have the best possible pilgrimage through life, we need to have the same kind of relationship with Christ that I had with Father Evans—a humble reliance on his judgment, to place our total trust in him, to accept his wisdom and knowledge and understanding, to rely on him for insight and guidance, and to allow him to be our tour guide through life.

But Christ wants to be more than just a tour guide. He wants to be our traveling companion and good friend as well.

On our trek through Europe, one of the highlights every day was to relax at night, after a hard day of touring, with a good meal and a great bottle of wine. Let me think for a second now—a bottle each night for twenty-one nights is twenty-one bottles. At twenty bucks a bottle, that's $420! Awful! Oh well, I'll only be in Europe once, and it was well worth it. We would get a little slap-happy, tell our favorite anecdotes for the day, talk about our lives for a little bit, tell a few jokes, and make plans for the next day.

That's a good model for what Mass should be all about. Christ is our traveling companion on our journey through life. The highlight of our travels should be our friendship with him. He desires to sit down and have a meal with us on a regular basis—to drink some wine, be filled with joy, and discuss the ups and downs of our lives together.

Mass on Sunday is a great place for us to thank Christ for our existence, to review the events of the past week, and to make plans together for how we want to live in the future.

But there is more to the Eucharist than just a plain meal. We are not just eating together. Christ is saying that he loves us so much that he wants to come into our lives and be part of who we are, to be present with us in all we do. And we, in return, are saying that we love Christ so much that we want to come into his life, to be present with him, to be part of his plan, and to help him do his work in the world.

The Eucharist is also much more than just a private relationship between an individual and Jesus Christ. It is a relationship between Christ and all of humanity. The body of Christ includes all of us together, becoming one in the Holy Spirit. This meal of the Eucharist is shared by all of us together. In Paul's letter to the Corinthians, he encourages the people of God to come together in love, friendship, and mutual respect, and to put aside their petty differences, and be of one mind, heart, and body.

On our trip to Europe, a little coincidence occurred that made me very happy. It turned out that we toured exactly four countries: Austria, Switzerland, France, and Germany. Here's the coincidence: on our first Saturday night we were in Salzburg, Austria, so we were able to attend the weekend Mass there at the beautiful cathedral. A few days later, on the feast of the Ascension, we were in Lucerne,

Switzerland, and we attended Mass at the equally beautiful Cathedral of St. Leodegard. The next Saturday evening we were in Avignon, France, and enjoyed Mass in French at the Church of St. Didymus. And finally, on the feast of Pentecost, we were treated to a grand liturgy of confirmation by the bishop in the awesome cathedral in Cologne, Germany.

So we were in four countries, each on a different feast day, and in so doing celebrated a major Mass in each country. Of course, these Masses were said in French and German, and it was frustrating to be unable to understand the homilies.

But the one universal thing was the sign of peace. When you turn to the people near you and receive a friendly smile and a warm handshake, it doesn't matter what language you speak. The gestures of friendship and love are always understandable without words. It is like the first Pentecost when the apostles could be understood by people of every race and tongue.

Another unmistakable ceremony is the Communion procession in which people come together from all over the world. They come forward in unity of faith and with the shared intent to be the Body of Christ. No words were necessary there either.

It all reminds us of the universal events of Jesus' own life: born a human being as a baby in a manger, curing people of illnesses, forgiving people of their sins, and suffering and dying on the cross for our salvation. There is no need for language at the center of our faith. Christ's actions speak for themselves and create an overwhelming depth of emotion and a personal bond that can be understood easily, no matter what our race or culture may be.

We are eternally grateful to Christ for all he has done for humankind as a whole, and for each one of us in particular. The word "Eucharist" is an ancient Greek word which means "thanksgiving." We come together this evening in a spirit of thankfulness to share a feast with our redeemer and friend, to allow him to come into our lives, and to commit ourselves to helping him build up the Body of Christ throughout the world.

Delivered at the Church of St. John in Grand Marais on the Feast of Corpus Christi June 21, 1992

The Key to Prayer

Would you like to hear about one of the biggest coincidences of my life? Last Sunday I had not yet read the readings for this week, so I had absolutely no idea of what they were about. I was driving alone in my car, listening to the Twins' game, and utterly depressed because they were losing to Baltimore, 5-0. So I turned to God in prayer and said, "Lord, help the Twins come back and win this game." Just then, they scored a run to make it 5-1.

All of a sudden the bases were loaded, with two outs, and Kent Hrbek was at bat. I prayed again, "Lord, help Herbie get a two run single!" But he hit a weak pop fly to shallow right center field to end the inning. "Thanks a lot, God!" I said.

But the Twins kept chipping away and, two innings later, the score was 5-3. Again the bases were loaded, with Kent Hrbek at the plate, and only one out this time. The thought of this gospel passage came into my head and I prayed, "Lord, you told us to be persistent in prayer and you would answer us. Well, I'm still begging! Help Hrbek get a two-run single!" He hit a foul pop-up for out number two.

"Thanks a lot, God!" I prayed. "I'm asking for an egg here and you're giving me a scorpion!" With two outs and the bases still loaded, Chili Davis came to the plate. "I refuse to give up, God! You said you'd answer my prayers if I begged until you got sick of me! Please help Chili hit a two-run single!"

Bam! There it went, and the game was tied. "Thank you, God!" I said. Then, with a man on third base, and Brian Harper at bat, in the spirit of Abraham, I prayed, "Lord, dare I presume upon your good will again? Let not my Lord grow impatient if I go on. Please help Harper get the game-winning hit!" BAM! Twins win, 7-5.

Well, I was overjoyed, and when I reached home and read the readings for this Sunday, I was grateful to God for giving me some instantaneous homily material. Victory is sweet. I was so elated that my prayer echoed the words of today's psalmist: "Lord, on the day

I called for help, you answered me.''

But does the Lord always grant exactly what we ask? No way! We all know that he does not. All our prayers are not answered in the way we would like. Last night I prayed just as hard. This time it was the Boston fans' turn to be heard. The Twins blew a lead to lose 5-4, and Oakland came from behind to beat Toronto 6-5. So who knows?

The same psalm continues, ''When I called, you answered me. You built up strength within me!'' That, in my opinion, is the key to prayer. God will give us the strength we need to handle any situation in our lives—if we trust in his goodness and love.

Does Jesus promise to bring victory to the Twins in today's Gospel if we pray hard enough? No! But he does promise that God will send the Holy Spirit if we ask. The Spirit gives us courage, insight, and the strength to endure. The Spirit gives us the understanding to realize that athletic victories and glory are so transient that they have very little significance in the spiritual life, especially when compared to our eternal salvation. The Holy Spirit is the answer to all our prayers.

Let me put it to you this way. Let's say that God would give you a choice between two things: you could either have one million dollars a year for the rest of your life, or you could have the spiritual gift of being totally contented in any situation, no matter what happens to you in life.

I bet that most people would choose the million bucks, even though the second gift is worth a lot more. We really don't know what is best for us. But God, as a loving father, has our best interests at heart.

Anthony Padovano writes, ''God is not someone who grants our wishes; he is someone who fulfills our hopes.''

Oscar Wilde put it another way: ''When the gods want to punish us, they give us what we ask for.''

To me, the key to understanding prayer lies in the second line of the Lord's Prayer: ''Thy kingdom come; thy will be done!'' It's the same basic prayer that Jesus said in the garden before his death. He wanted the cup to pass and to let him go on living. God wanted him to save the world. Jesus ultimately got his prayer answered when he arose from the dead to *eternal* life. But his prayers were answered by a difficult course of events that only God, in his wisdom, could understand.

The Our Father is a perfect prayer given to us by the perfect prayor just after he was engaged in deep prayer himself. The early Fathers of the Church said that it should be prayed by every Christian at least three times every day.

God is our father, the head of the family. It is his kingdom in which we reside. He is in charge. He has everything under control. We must be obedient to his will. He gives all and forgives all.

If we truly believe in those words, then we can be at peace no matter what happens to us in life. True prayer is the humility to surrender to God's providence and to trust in his desire for our welfare. His plan is for all of us to share in his boundless love forever.

The Lord's Prayer teaches us humble reliance and a spirit of acceptance and gratitude for whatever comes our way, even when it seems contrary to our prayers.

I had one of the greatest religious experiences of my life last month when I went to Lourdes. Having untreatable cancer has given me a special appreciation for God's gift of life. Consequently, I don't want it to end. So I naturally went to Lourdes with a strong desire to be cured.

We arrived in Lourdes by train, and I was immediately captivated by its spectacular mountain setting. It is a beautiful city. As we walked through the pearly gates into a gigantic courtyard full of beautiful flowers and statues, I was floored by a spiritual sense of God's presence everywhere. There was no commercialism. That was kept outside the gates. Inside was only peace and love. The church rose above the surroundings in the distance, hovering over the entire area like a fountain of God's graces. The church looked like the church in Fantasyland. I felt like I was in the Magic Kingdom of the Catholic Church. Mass was celebrated about twenty times every day in different chapels and in many languages. It was nice to understand the homily for a change. The priest talked about accepting our difficulties and remembering that we don't have any more suffering than any of the early martyrs.

There was also a beautiful underground church with twenty-nine colorful, stained glass windows depicting the fourteen stations of the cross and each of the fifteen mysteries of the rosary. I had just bought sixteen rosaries to bring home for the people of our parish who have cancer. (I apologize to those I missed. It's amazing how many people have cancer, and my memory is not perfect.) I took out one of the rosaries and walked around to each window, having a great time praying all fifteen mysteries and seeing them come to life in front of me through the windows.

Then I went out into a huge garden on a high hill that had life-size stations of the cross to walk through. It was wonderful to follow the steps of Christ. My prayer became one with his prayer in the garden: "Your will, not mine, be done!"

I then went down to the grotto, blessed myself and all the rosaries in the waters of Lourdes, and composed this little prayer:

> Thank you, Lord, for this beautiful day, and for getting us safely to Lourdes. I ask you to bless these rosaries. May they be a sign to those who use them of your love and the love of your mother, Mary. If it be your will, free us from our sicknesses, but, above all, grant us peace and a true acceptance of our sufferings. In any case, help us to love you with all our hearts, through all our difficulties. We make this prayer through Jesus Christ our Lord. Amen.

I left that place with a sense of peace and an awareness of God's love surrounding me. To me, it does not matter whether I live or die because, either way, as St. Paul says in the second reading, "Christ lives in me through my baptism, and he will bring me to eternal life in his presence!"

Richard Viladesau suggests that "the proper religious attitude is the acceptance of God's will; the proper kind of prayer is praising God for whatever he wills. . . . For many Christians, the notion of 'prayer' that is unconsciously taken for granted is almost the opposite: not submission to God's will, but the effort to change God's will and to get him to submit to our will or to fulfill our agenda." The prayer of petition is then "a matter of making ourselves—like Jesus—the means of God's transformation of the world in his Spirit, the spirit of love."*

As I left the Lourdes grotto, I came to a lovely statue of Mary, with outstretched arms, and surrounded by a small field of white roses. It looked like a mystical vision of heaven come to life. My final prayer was, "Lord, if you want to heal me, I would not object, but, if not, please prepare me to go to Heaven." I walked out of the courtyard

---

*Richard Viladesau, "Seventeenth Sunday of the Year," *The Word In and Out of Season: Homilies for the Sundays of Ordinary Time, Cycle C* (Paulist, 1991) 58–61. Quoted with the author's permission.

with a feeling of total peace, knowing that God has my best interests
at heart.

Delivered at the Church of St. John in Grand Marais
on the Seventeenth Sunday of the Church Year
July 26, 1992

The Communion of Saints

You renew the Church in every age
by raising up men and women outstanding in holiness,
living witnesses of your unchanging love.
They inspire us by their heroic lives,
and help us by their constant prayers
to be the living sign of your saving power.

Preface of Holy Men and Women II

Sharing an Absolutely Mystical Experience with God

In today's gospel Christ works a miracle by feeding five thousand people with five loaves and two fish. The mind boggles. It sounds like my mother trying to stretch the food supplies at a Nolan-Hollenhorst reunion.

Everybody having his fill reminds me of the rehearsal dinner at Dennis and Elena McGrann's wedding a few years back in which an Italian couple served us loads of food in seven or eight courses. They kept coming back to us with more and more food over a four-hour period. I was sitting across from Marie who stated, with emphasis, "Well, I don't need to eat again for another three weeks."

If Jesus had that much food on hand, he probably could have fed all of Minneapolis and St. Paul and still had enough food left over to feed the Minnesota Vikings' defensive line.

When I was a kid growing up, I knew that my parents loved me because they provided food and made my meals for me. Eating is a basic human need, and I am grateful to my parents for satisfying my hunger. All of us can share that sense of gratitude to our parents for their generosity in sustaining us through childhood. They gave us life in the first place; and, by providing for our needs, they were telling us, "we like what we created, and we want you to go on living."

With the miracle of the loaves and fishes, Christ shows God's love in the same way. He is a caring father who communicates his love by sustaining us with food. Therefore, when we eat we are sharing an absolutely mystical experience with God.

It is as though he were saying to us, "I created you! Your life is very valuable to me! Eat the food I provide and go on living!"

We should always have a sense of humble reliance and gratitude to God for the food we eat. It is he who nourishes, gives us strength, and sustains our lives. We are all grateful to God for the many gifts he has given us—life, food, family, friends, faith, love, and hope.

The gospel today carries the subtle hint that God has put enough resources in our world to provide for every human being on earth. But, if we want to have enough to go around for everyone, we, like God, need to have generous spirits. If we are selfish and hoard our possessions, many in the world will be deprived of their basic human needs. If we share what we have, all can be satisfied. When we partake in the Eucharist, Christ calls us to a spirit of self-sacrifice—to give of ourselves to others.

Today, we gather together to honor one such giving spirit: Marie Adair. The people of St. Francis Parish would like to express their appreciation to Marie for her generosity in giving land to St. Francis school to help make a nice playground for the children.

I was happy and proud to hear that St. Francis Parish was planning to honor Marie in this way because she has been very generous to her relatives as well. So it gives us a chance to thank her, too.

My mother says that Marie has been especially generous with her time and resources when it comes to children. She devoted much of her life to teaching children with learning disabilities. I've always thought that most teachers must be generous at heart, since they are paid only about half as much money as they are worth to our society.

Marie, along with Eula Michael, volunteered her time to the Campfire Girls, and Marie was the camp director at Clearwater Lake.

I know Marie was generous to me when I was a child. She has a special place in my heart because she is also my godmother. She was a good choice for me because she inspired a sense of spiritual awe in me. My mother used to tell stories about Marie's father, Uncle Sam. I always associated him with the spirit of America because of his name, because he was a pioneer around Gull Lake, and because the name of our road was Samadair Road. When I learned that Marie was Uncle Sam's child, it was as though she was the daughter of a legend, and she herself became a legend in my mind.

Marie, too, was a pioneer on Gull Lake. When my brother, Jim, and I were ten years old, she invited us to spend a couple of weeks with her out in the primitive wilderness that was Gull Lake in those days. She had a log cabin with a hand pump on the side of the sink to draw water from the well, and an outhouse called "The Star."

Marie has always loved the wilderness, and all the plant and animal life it contains. At the cabin she used to have a garden that took up much of her time. She shared her horticultural expertise with the city of Brainerd. When she and Eula were members of the Garden

Club, they helped to plant flowering crab trees all around town. You can still see them growing in front of the post office, city hall, and the courthouse.

Marie and Eula also belonged to the Thursday Club. Jim and I thought it was pretty funny when they took us to one of their meetings on Wednesday afternoon.

Marie was generous with her land at Gull Lake as well. She gave one hundred feet of shoreline to the Gull-Love Marina so a channel could be dredged to connect the two lakes. She shared some of her land with our family and others. Lots and lots of people are now able to enjoy the lakes and woods that have given value to her life.

Marie is now ninety-five years old. That is incredible. She has put in almost a whole century in this garden of earth. Maybe her longevity can be attributed to her generosity. She is not quite as active as she used to be, but, as her presence here today indicates, she still loves to get out and be with people. And we are all happy to be with you, Marie, to celebrate this special moment together.

I just celebrated a major milestone in my life in April, my fortieth birthday. I can't believe I am that old. You know, when I was one year old, my parents were about forty times older than I was. Now they are less than twice as old as I am. I guess I am getting older a lot faster than Marie is.

At my birthday party in Grand Marais, a lady gave me this beautiful rock for a present. On it she had painted some words that call to mind the message of today's gospel: "Love is a basket with five loaves and two fishes—it's never enough until you start to give it away."

In the spirit of the gospel, in the spirit of our celebration of Marie's generosity, and in the spirit of the message written on this rock, I would like to give it to Marie in honor of this day.

Delivered at the Church of St. Francis in Brainerd, Minnesota,
at a Mass to honor Marie Adair
August 5, 1990

Pain Is God's Megaphone to Rouse a Deaf World

I was just inducted as an Elk in November. It is a joy for me to be asked to speak in behalf of our departed brothers. We gather today to honor our brothers who have died this past year.

Many of you who have been Elks for a long time probably got to know these men quite well over the years. It is hard to say good-bye to them, and you must suffer at the loss of good friends. They were an important part of your lives, and now they are gone. We long to see them again, to be physically with them, to talk with them, and share ourselves with them. But all we can do is to rely on our memories of them.

The death of loved ones has always been a plague to humankind. History is full of examples of the grief caused by death. The Bible records that, one thousand years before Christ, David mourned the loss of his friend Jonathan. Remember the legend of Orpheus and Eurydice in which he went into hell after his beloved to bring her back? Jesus wept at the death of Lazarus.

The Bible is filled with stories of widows grieving for their husbands. Today, we remember not only our departed brothers, we remember their widows as well. Widows are often forgotten after their husbands die. We Elks want you ladies to know that you are in our hearts and prayers. And remember also that God has not forgotten you. He is with you as a source of comfort and strength in this time of need.

We must endure our pain of loss and go on living. The late book editor, Hiram Hayden, once asked the poet Melville Crane, a wealthy man in his nineties, the secret of his longevity. When Crane realized that the question was sincere, he paused and replied, "I have learned to live with pain." It takes time to learn to live with pain, especially the pain of loss. We will never find any better way to help us grow in either wisdom or holiness, nor is there any better teacher to help us embrace our own inevitable death with a spirit of peace.

C.S. Lewis observed, "God whispers to us in our pleasures, speaks to us in our conscience, but shouts to us in our pain. It is his megaphone to rouse a deaf world.'' We learn to live with pain not by denying it, pretending that it does not exist. Nor do we live with it by fighting it. The pain of loss is there, and we must learn to embrace it.

By learning to accept the pain and live with it, we can learn much from the death of a loved one. Death teaches us that life is a very precious gift. Even if we live to be one hundred, life passes by awfully fast. It is such a transient thing. We must always appreciate that gift of life. Never take it for granted. We must make the best of each moment. We should live as if each moment might be our last, and make every moment count.

From what I have seen of the Elks, they do make life meaningful. They do make it count. Elks enjoy life, with social functions and celebrations of all kinds. Their respect for life is shown by their concern for others. I've been reading out of the handbook, *What it Means to Be an Elk,* and was immediately impressed with the first paragraph. It states, ''The declared purposes of the Elks are to practice its four cardinal virtues: Charity, Justice, Brotherly love, and Fidelity; to promote the welfare and enhance the happiness of its members; to quicken the spirit of American patriotism; and to cultivate good fellowship.'' These are noble principles, and if we live them out, we get a worthwhile sense of our lives, and we can die happy.

We honor our departed brothers today, and trust that these are the virtues by which they lived their lives. But death is not just a painful thing for us, but a joyful thing as well. I think that in our culture, we have placed too much emphasis on death as a thing to be feared, to guard against, to avoid at all costs.

In many cultures, death was a great honor, and something to be celebrated with joy. Autumn reminds us that death can be a beautiful thing. Leaves, as they die, turn brilliant colors and brighten up our world. Why is death beautiful? Because death is not the end of life, but a new beginning. Resurrection. Sharing eternal life with God. At a time like this, it is good to remember the words of Jonathan Swift about death: ''It is impossible that anything so natural, so necessary and so universal as death should ever have been designed by Providence as an evil to mankind.''

Our faith does not deny the pain of death nor does it attempt to explain the suffering, but it does give meaning to pain and suffering and death. God does not abandon those who trust him. His love for us transcends death and enables us to endure the pain of loss and continue to embrace each new day in a spirit of hope and peace, confident that this life flows through death into eternal life.

The approaching first Sunday of Advent is a good time to celebrate a memorial service. We are all waiting with anticipation for the second coming of Christ. Our departed brothers no longer have to wait. They have met Christ, and are sharing new life with him. The Elk's antlers are a sign of the resurrection and new life.

Presented to the Grand Marais Elks.
Undated.

An Old Grain of Wheat, but a Great Grain

Family, and relatives, and friends: some of you come from quite a distance to be here. And it is nice that we could all get together today on this sad but also happy occasion to remember and pray for Gramma. I usually preach for only about two minutes at a funeral, but I feel so privileged to talk about Gramma that I hope you will not mind my taking a few more minutes today. Josephine Hollenhorst was a great lady who lived a long and good life of ninety-two years. It's amazing to me to think about how long a span of time that is. She almost made it to see Halley's Comet twice. Most of us will be lucky if we live to see it even once.

Gramma is being buried on the same day that the Columbia is making its third voyage. Yet she was around when the Wright Brothers made their first historic flight. She lived through the Spanish-American War, World War I, and sent her sons off to World War II. Thank God they all returned in good health.

Even though Gramma did live a long time, life never seems long enough for one we love, and love her we all did. It's hard not to love one who is so full of love herself. She had a wonderful family of ten children, forty grandchildren, and nineteen great-grandchildren. I think that between her and her ten brothers, they were responsible for populating at least half of Stearns County.

Speaking as a grandson, I know that she knew us all. She cared for and loved each one of us. It was pretty obvious to me that her family was the most important thing in her life.

In the last few years, Gramma suffered quite a bit. Her children had the opportunity to pay her back by taking care of her. Everyone helped to some extent, but, being such a spread out family, some did more than others. All of us are grateful to Aunt Lorraine and Uncle Art for their care in past years. We are grateful to Aunt Virginia and Uncle Pat, and to Aunt Elaine and Uncle Ron. But we are especially grateful to Aunt Edith and Uncle Tom who cared for Gramma the last three years of her life.

I know that for some of you this is a difficult time. It is hard to say good-bye to a loved one. But it is also a joyful time as well, and the last few days have really brought back a lot of warm memories to me. Thinking about Gramma has made me feel like I am ten years old again. The only bad memory I have about Gramma is with regard to one occasion when she was baby-sitting with us. I was being extremely obnoxious one night, and she started chasing me around the house with a belt. But that is as far as it went, for when she caught up to me, she whipped out a deck of cards and we had a great game of cribbage. Being a card-playing fanatic, I think I am qualified to make judgments about other people's card-playing abilities and, in my book, Gramma was the greatest pinochle and cribbage player who ever lived. She enjoyed teaching the game to others, and she always won. Somehow, though, she always made you feel good about losing to her.

Some of the best memories of my life have to do with going to the lake in Brainerd, and with stopping at Gramma's on the way. She would always greet us at the door with a smile and offer us some of her homemade bread. Two great recipes for bread have come out of St. Cloud. Most people know about how good St. John's Bread is. But we in Gramma's family know about an even better brand. I think the greatest thing that ever happened in our family was when Mom somehow got her hands on Gramma's secret recipe.

I'll just mention one more great memory I have of Gramma. When she used to stay with us, she would deep-fry pieces of bread dough and then dip them in sugar. Then she tried to put them on the dining table, but they never got that far, as we gobbled them up so fast that there was never any trace of their existence. It must have been rewarding for Gramma to see that bread dough transformed into smiles on our faces. To me, that is symbolic of who Gramma was.

Now that she is dead, there will remain very little of her physical existence. She lived such a simple life. She had so few possessions. And yet she left so much in the love she had for all of us. Her physical existence has transformed into a warmth in all of our hearts. We, as Christians, can be happy for Gramma today. God blessed her with a good and full life, and we know that death is not the end of life. It is a new beginning. As St. Paul reminds us, when Gramma was baptized, she began a spiritual relationship with Jesus Christ. Because she died with Christ, she will also share in his resurrection.

The Gospel today points out that unless the grain of wheat falls to the earth and dies, it remains just a grain of wheat. But if it dies, it produces much fruit. Gramma was an old grain of wheat, but she was a great grain of wheat. Let us pray that God will welcome her into his kingdom.

Delivered at the Funeral Mass for Josephine Meinz Hollenhorst
St. Mary's Cathedral, St. Cloud, Minnesota
March 22, 1982

Christmas and Beyond

*Paul VI found the spirit of Advent
expressed in words first uttered
long before Christ:
"From the unreal,
lead me to the real;
from darkness,
lead me to light;
from death,
lead me to immortality."*

Paul VI: The First Modern Pope
Peter Hebblethwaite

Christ's Light Shining in Every Situation

On Monday I had to do some last minute shopping in Duluth. And I must say, I surprised myself with the amount of patience I exhibited. I did, however, ace out one lady for a parking place. I hope she will forgive me in the spirit of Christmas joy.

The hassle of preparation is all worth it because, well, here we are celebrating another Christmas. And I, for one, am mighty happy to be here, for we have a beautiful crib and tree, parish volunteers who never cease to inspire profound gratitude in me, lush chrysanthemums with a refreshing aroma, heart-warming music from a dedicated choir, friendly, familiar, smiling faces, some of which we haven't seen for quite some time, lights and colorful decorations, satisfying food and beverages, a furnace that still works, and a God who continues to love us and amaze us with his miracles.

Today we celebrate his greatest miracle, the virgin birth of our Lord and Savior Jesus Christ, "Emmanuel," which means "God is with us." And tonight we can really feel his presence through the warmth and love of this special Christmas mass.

An article appeared a while back in the *Minneapolis Star Tribune* summarizing the results of a survey that was taken among Minnesota school children. They were asked whether or not they believed in God and, if so, to give their impressions of what he was like.

I'd like to read four of the answers which relate to the Christmas season. Eight-year-old Rebecca's response was this: "Yes, there is a God. He has a beard and looks over us. God has this TV screen and sees everything we do. He knows when we've been bad or good, so be good for goodness sake. The angels gave God the TV screen for his birthday."

It sounds like Rebecca is combining a few different legends. I guess now we know how God celebrates Christmas. He plays *Nintendo* like everybody else.

Seventeen-year-old Marie responded with a little more mature answer: "Why should I believe in God? We are told that he is good, yet look at all the bad things that happen in the world. If there is a God, why did he let my friend get run over by a car? People say he is our Savior. Then why is there all this pain in the world?''

That's a touching, sincere thought, and I appreciate it, especially coming from a young person who is searching for the truth. But I must say that I do not agree with her. I have found suffering in my life. But, I have also found God in that suffering. The more we mature, the more we realize that religion can never be an escape from the pain of living. We all have suffering to endure. It is all part of life.

Who is the most religious person you can think of? Jesus? Mary? Could they escape suffering? No way! Jesus died a horrible death on the cross, and Mary had to stand there watching as her son died in front of her. Yet they both saw the love of God shining through all that they endured.

I think what Marie needs to learn is that God will come to anyone who opens his or her heart. His presence can turn the worst suffering into a kind of joy. With his love in our hearts, we can endure anything. The mature faith sees Christ's light shining in every situation, pleasant or painful.

I am amazed at the number of people who have gone through tragedy and, when interviewed on TV, suggest that if they didn't have God to fall back to and rely on for emotional security, they would never make it through their difficulties.

That brings us to fifth grade Laura's response to the survey question. She says, ''Sometimes I think of God as a 911 God. When I need help, I call him and he always seems to be there!'' Laura, to my way of thinking, is right on the money.

If I were to answer the survey question myself, I would say, God so loved the world that he sent his only son, Jesus Christ, into it to be our Savior. The qualities of this God-Savior are compassion, mercy, the forgiveness of sinners, love of all people, especially the poor. This God shows concern for the sick and the suffering, gives strength for the weak, justice for the oppressed, and brings peace of mind for the weary, the restless, and the worried.

I would go on to state that Jesus Christ, the Son of God, loves us personally so much that he died for us on the cross and rose from the dead, so that he could live with us and we could live with him forever. He gives us his own body and blood to eat and drink whenever we celebrate the Eucharist together. He is the Prince of Peace, the Light of Justice, who wants everyone on earth to live in his kingdom as loving brothers and sisters.

One final response to the survey comes from ten-year-old Rod who says, "I still don't know where God lives. Why doesn't he come down here and live with us?" Well, I guess that's what this Christmas season is all about. God was born of the Virgin Mary in a cave filled with animals in Bethlehem on Christmas Eve almost two thousand years ago. And the baby's name is Jesus, also known as Emmanuel, which means "God is with us!"

Christmas is all about God becoming human, the eternal word of God becoming flesh and blood, and dwelling among us. The Son of God becoming the son of Mary, true God and true man. I'm getting to sound too much like the creed. The point is, we don't have to try to get to know, love, and serve some distant mystical being who is way off in another dimension or way up there, out of touch with our existence.

Our God lives down here on earth, through the gift of the Holy Spirit. Right here in our hearts, if we accept him and allow him to dwell within us.

My wish is that all of you may have a very Merry Christmas, filled with peace and joy. And may you also be filled with the love of Christ our Savior, now and throughout the new year. Amen.

Delivered at the Church of St. John in Grand Marais on Christmas
December 25, 1992

Coming Together Without Prejudice

Virgil wrote in the Aeneid, ''I fear Greeks even when they bring gifts.'' In today's gospel King Herod is suspicious of three wise men journeying to his country with gifts for the Christ child. So he plays some games with them, pretending to welcome them, and then conniving behind their backs.

We may be a bit like Herod when strangers enter our lives, when foreigners enter our communities, when new people try to become part of our cliques. I was disgusted this last Halloween when I heard on the news that a foreign exchange student, who was out trick-or-treating for the first time, was gunned down and killed for trespassing on a man's front lawn.

Last spring, I was in Cologne, Germany, and there was graffiti spray-painted all over the walls telling Turks and other foreigners that, unless they get out of their country and go home, terrible things would start happening to them.

Well, I guess those ugly, terrible things have begun to happen, after I left, fortunately. It is ironic that such a spirit would be hovering over Cologne. It is such a beautiful city on the Rhine River, which itself was originally settled by foreigners as a frontier outpost of the Roman empire. It also has the most magnificent cathedral I have ever seen, dedicated to the memory of the three Wise Men. Their relics are supposedly contained within the church.

The symbolism of the Magi is that they were people of every race and tongue, coming together without prejudice and worshiping the baby Jesus in a spirit of brotherhood. If we want that spirit of all people living together in peace as God's family, we are going to have to do better at eliminating bigotry and prejudice. And it all begins at home, in the way we treat those in our own communities.

Do we encourage cliques or social clubs that deliberately exclude whole categories of people? Do we taunt outsiders and make them feel unwanted? Do we support hazings and code reds and initiation rituals that demean the value of human life and dignity? Or do we

31

welcome those who seem a bit foreign to our way of thinking, inviting them to become a part of our group?

Jesus is the Prince of Peace. It is his desire to be the savior of every person on earth. It is God's desire that every human being be his adopted son or daughter. It was in that spirit that three gentile kings traveled thousands of miles from different corners of the world to bow down to a Jewish baby.

Tradition has it that one of those kings came from Ethiopia. Today, our nation has traveled to the neighborhood of Ethiopia, to a county called Somalia, bearing gifts for their children as emissaries of peace and justice, to establish a brotherhood and sisterhood among all God's children.

I hope that this cooperation is a sign of better things to come in the world.

May Christ help the people on this planet become one family in God's love. Amen.

Delivered at the Church of St. John in Grand Marais on the Feast of the Epiphany January 3, 1993

PRAYER TO OUR LADY

In Her Title of La Conquistadora

O Lady Conqueror, promised in Eden as the Woman whose Seed would crush the Serpent's head, help us to conquer evil in our midst and in our hearts, with the grace of your Son, Jesus Christ, Our God and Our Saviour!

O Lady Conqueror, through your Motherhood of Our Saviour, Who is True God and True Man, help us overcome all errors regarding His Person and the Church that He founded for His Glory and our salvation!

O Lady Conqueror, through Jesus, who is the Prince of Peace and our Universal King, convert by His Divine Power, which is above all human might, the infidels and all the enemies of His Peace!

O Lady Conqueror, do conquer our hearts with your Immaculate loveliness, so that drawn from sinful ways to the precepts of your Son, we may glorify Him in this life, and, victoriously come to know Him, with you and all the Saints, forever in the next! Amen.

Robert F. Sanchez
Archibishop of Santa Fe

Air Traffic Control
and Our Relationship with God

I just came back from a great trip out west to visit my brother John in Salt Lake City. He and his wife Swantje are celebrating the baptism of their daughter, Annie, today, which is very appropriate, as today is the Feast of the Baptism of the Lord. In the gospel today we read about Jesus being baptized by John in the Jordan River. It reminds us about how each one of us has been baptized into God's family: we are his adopted children and have become brothers and sisters of Jesus Christ.

On my trip to Utah, the weather was awful—sleet and snow everywhere. The sleet would drop out of the sky and turn to ice on whatever it hit. This created very hazardous conditions in which to travel. At the Minneapolis airport, as we were waiting to take off, the wings became encased in ice and had to be passed through a steam bath before we could fly. We lined up on the runway again, and fire trucks came out and melted off the ice with steam.

Isn't that a lot like the sacrament of baptism? Since the time of Adam and Eve, our world has been in a kind of nasty environment of original sin. On our pilgrimage through life, we have to travel within this hostile atmosphere, which is not always supportive of a healthy life; and so, at the beginning of our journey, God comes to us in a spirit of love. He sends Christ, our savior, to give us a bath, to wash us clean of all the stuff that will hinder us from having a successful journey.

I was amazed by the efficiency of the general operation of the airport. We were in a line of ten planes. There must have been twenty fire trucks de-icing the wings. Planes were landing and taking off within seconds of each other on the same runway.

It was immediately obvious that there was a supreme will and authority directing all of this activity from the control tower high above us, organizing and channeling hundreds of vehicles into workable patterns on the ground and in the air. This supreme, guiding will was invisible, and all the pilots had to have faith that it was there. For this whole operation to work, it took every vehicle's driver to have a sense of teamwork with every other driver. They each had to put their total trust in the competence of the control tower personnel. They had to give the controllers their complete cooperation and obedience.

Isn't that the way it should be in our relationship with God? We need faith in his existence, trust in his guidance, and obedience to his will.

When we were baptized, we became part of a team—the People of God. He is the great coordinator, and we offer ourselves in service to his will to help his family of love, peace, and justice grow and flourish in this world.

The take-off from Minneapolis frightened me because halfway through the acceleration phase of the take-off, there was a great surge of braking power. I was certain we were about to collide with a landing plane. We came to a complete stop, and the pilot informed us that a cargo door was open. So we had to return and repeat the entire procedure, including the de-icing.

That was a symbolic reminder to me that baptism is a good start, but it is not magic. When we are washed clean, it doesn't guarantee perfection or total commitment to Christ throughout our lives. We have to keep renewing our allegiance to God. That is why we renew our baptismal promises every week at mass by reciting the creed together. It reminds us of our baptism and helps us to recommit ourselves to God.

I had the opportunity to accompany my brother John, a journalist, on a news story field trip out to Vernal, Utah, in the eastern Uinta mountain basin. Apparently, governmental flood control projects, combined with crop irrigation techniques, are causing a chemical called selenium to be leached out of the Mancos shale stratum and become concentrated into the streams, ponds, and marshes of the Stewart Lake Wildlife Management Area. Rangers showed us evidence that the selenium was causing birth defects in the beaks and wings of baby ducklings.

All this goes to show you how important the environment is in the development of the young. The environment is even more important for human beings who are so much more complex than birds. There is a whole spiritual dimension that we need to be concerned about. A healthy spiritual environment is essential for the complete development of our children. Baptism is a good beginning, but God doesn't do it alone. Parents, too, have a big responsibility to provide an atmosphere of loving support in the home. They must help their children to know of the loving God who is watching over them with a benevolent spirit. They have a savior in Jesus Christ who forgives our transgressions and makes us whole again.

Throughout this holiday season, we have been celebrating how God was born as a little baby. Mary and Joseph provided the healthy spiritual environment in which Jesus could grow to manhood. They must have done a great job. In the gospel we hear God say, "This is my beloved Son, in whom I am well pleased."

Today, we do not celebrate Jesus as a baby, or as a child, but as a mature adult, who commits himself to a life of service in God's kingdom.

Let us share his example, and resolve to do his work to help build up his kingdom of light, justice, and peace.

Delivered at the Church of St. John, Grand Marais,
on the Feast of the Baptism of the Lord
January 10, 1993

Why Not the Lion or the Tiger of God?

"Look there! The Lamb of God who takes away the sins of the world!" Made you look! If you aren't looking, turn around and catch a view of the beautiful stained glass window that Fr. Urban [Steiner, O.S.B., the former pastor] left our parish. We see John baptizing Jesus in the Jordan River. Jesus' baptism is a sign to us that God chose him to be our Savior. And that he called him to suffer and die for our sins. John mentions that God filled Jesus with the Holy Spirit to give him the strength, courage, and wisdom he needed to carry out his mission.

"Behold the Lamb of God!" he says, the Lamb of God! We take those words for granted. Since we were little children, we have heard those words at least four times every Sunday: Lamb of God, you take away the sins of the world, have mercy on us! Lamb of God, you take away the sins of the world, have mercy on us! Lamb of God, you take away the sins of the world, grant us peace! This is the Lamb of God, who takes away the sins of the world. Happy are those who are called to his supper.

Why the Lamb of God?—a weak, mousy, little animal? Why not the lion or the tiger of God? A mighty force who will champion the cause of God's justice with a great power? Instead, we refer to him as a helpless lamb—a meek, little animal, passively waiting to be slaughtered.

The lamb, in the Jewish faith, is a symbol of sacrifice. Remember the story of Cain and Abel. Cain offered up some grain to God in gratitude for a good harvest. And Abel killed a lamb, and offered it up in gratitude to God, giving back a small portion of the flock that God had first given. Of the two offerings, God was most pleased with Abel's gift of a first-born lamb.

The tradition continues with Abraham. He was about to offer up his first-born son Isaac when the angel suggested that he offer up a lamb instead. Since these early days, on a regular basis, the priests would kill a lamb on the altar, offer it up to God, and sprinkle its blood on the people as a sacrifice to take away their sins.

And that brings us to the great feast of the Jewish faith, Passover. The Israelites, of course, were slaves in Egypt. What did they do the night on which God came to be their Savior, to rescue them from Pharaoh, to lead them out of Egypt into the Promised Land? They killed a lamb, ate it, and painted its blood on the doors of their houses so that the angel of God would pass over, passing them by without danger on his way to kill the first born of all Egyptians.

The people won their freedom, and every year since then, they sacrifice a first-born lamb to God in gratitude. When they eat the lamb, it brings back the great victory that God had won for them, and it reminds them that they are his people and that they entered into a covenant to live by his will.

Today, John calls Jesus the Lamb—the Paschal Lamb of the Jewish feast of Passover. He is going to offer himself up to God as the perfect sacrifice, slain on the altar of the cross. His blood will be sprinkled on the entire world, as a sin offering, to free us from the bondage of evil in the world.

In the same way that the Jews sacrifice a lamb every year and eat it, so we renew Jesus' sacrifice on the cross at every mass. When we eat the body and drink the blood of Christ, we celebrate the great victory that Jesus won for us over sin. This is an agreement our parents made for us when we were baptized and an agreement we make for ourselves when we are confirmed.

And what is God's will? It is that we try to be like Jesus—a people of love, a people serving humanity, a people suffering for others. We are to be, as Isaiah says in the first reading, "Suffering servants, called to renew the world."

Like Jesus, we received the gift of the Holy Spirit when we were baptized and confirmed. The Spirit gives us strength, courage, and wisdom to help us carry out our task of being Christ's ambassadors of love in the world.

There's a nice little message for young people hidden in the readings today. Isaiah says, "It is too little, God says, for you to be my servants, to raise up my people, and rescue them. I will make you a light to the nations, that my salvation may reach to the ends of the earth!"

Older folks get kind of sedentary, sort of stuck in their ways. We tend to settle down and stay fixed. But young people are more mobile. They are bursting with energy and a desire to travel and see the world. You are in a unique position to get out and see people of foreign lands. Lots of young people serve God by being a light to the nations. Wherever you go, you can bring Christ with you, and be a light for others. Some do it on their own. Others join established programs. When I was in college, I took a summer off from work to be part of the Glenmary Missionary Program in the Appalachian Mountains. It was one of the greatest experiences of my life, and I am always grateful that I did it. Some young people join the Peace Corps and help less fortunate people in the world to find a bit of justice in their lives. Every year our young people are fortunate to meet twelve young people on the National Evangelization Team (NET) who come to us from all over the country. They have offered a year of their lives to go on the road for God. They always seem to be excited and fulfilled in their missionary work.

This year we see Dr. Dahlman taking some years out of his medical practice here at home to serve some of the disadvantaged people of Africa. My advice to the young people of our parish is to take advantage of this time in your life, this time just after graduating from high school. Put some excitement into your lives. If you think you might like to do something like that, I can get you information about such organized programs.

I really like the opportunities that Marilyn Duffy is providing to the young people this year to help them think about more than just our own little community. The students are helping to support two children in the foreign lands of Indonesia and Ecuador. And, in addition to that, as I was thinking about what to say today, three organizations popped into my mind: Duluth Entertainment and Convention Center (DECC), Teens Encounter Christ (TEC), and Trek.

Last week at the DECC in Duluth, young people from our parish met with kids from all over the diocese to build a wider community, and to celebrate life. On TEC weekends, young people go on retreat for a few days, and discover a community of love that is made up of kids from lots of different parishes from all over our diocese. And next summer, many of our teenagers will be trekking to Denver to see the Pope, and to meet kids from all over the country. This is not just their trip though. They are representatives of our whole parish, and I would like to see us all get behind them and support them with our prayers, and by helping them to raise money for the journey to cut down on the burden of expenses.

I think that in Grand Marais, being so far from civilization, we get sort of an isolated mentality both physically and spiritually. We forget that we are called to love as brothers and sisters.

Today, in the readings, we are offered a challenge. To support the worldwide efforts of the church to build up God's family of light, love, justice, and peace. We don't have to actually travel to other areas to be of service to the people in distant lands. We are members of a Church that is already reaching out. We need to support our Church with a positive attitude towards others, with our continual prayers, and with our financial support of its programs. Next week, we will be taking up a collection for the people of Latin America. Please give generously.

Delivered at the Church of St. John in Grand Marais
on the Second Sunday of the Church Year
January 17, 1993

Celebrating Light, Entering the Kingdom

Yesterday, I was driving home from Duluth and had a chance to listen to a story on Minnesota Public Radio about the village of Barrow, Alaska. The people there live in darkness for three months out of the year. The teacher of some grade-school children was talking about how depressing it gets living your days without the sun. It helped her to believe that one day the sun would rise again and the light would come back.

Yesterday was that day! And it was a very special day for the students in her class. The sun was about to return and they were all going outside to greet it and celebrate its arrival. When the sun rose, the children held up cards with messages of affection and sang together, "You are my sunshine, my only sunshine." What they had hoped for during those three long months of darkness had finally come to pass, and there was great rejoicing.

In today's gospel, and also from the book of Isaiah, we read these heartening words: "The people who walked in darkness have seen a great light; upon those who dwelt in the land of gloom, a light has shone. Oh, Lord, you have brought them abundant joy. For the yoke that burdened them, you have smashed, as on the day of Midian." In the gospel today, we see that long-awaited light rising and shining on the people of Israel who had been in darkness so long. Jesus is God's answer to the hopes of his people. He has sent the savior to them. Matthew says, "Jesus toured all of Galilee. He taught in their synagogues, proclaimed the good news of the Kingdom, and cured the people of every disease and illness." Bigger and bigger crowds gathered until, at one point, over five thousand people had come together on a mountain to hear Jesus speak his comforting words.

We, too, live in a world darkened by violence, poverty, injustice, hatred, war, famine, pestilence, disease, and death, not to mention loneliness, fear, worry, sadness, despair, and distress. We need the light of Christ just as much as the Israelites did two thousand years ago, both in our individual lives, and in the world as a whole.

40

This last week in which we celebrated the inauguration of President Clinton, we seemed to be like those early crowds who gathered around Jesus—even more excited, joy-filled, and hopeful. On that day 250,000 people came together as one on the Washington Mall. Millions more watched on TV, united as one nation, to hear the new president speak of wonderful things. We heard how we could change the world, make it a better place. It was much like Jesus telling us to change our hearts, because the kingdom of God is at hand. President Clinton tells us to be responsible and to sacrifice for the good of all. Jesus tells us to pick up our crosses and follow him, to be his responsible servants, and to love our neighbors as our own family. President Clinton makes promises, guaranteeing how life will be better if we work together in a spirit of cooperation.

Next week we will hear Jesus speak the beatitudes in the Sermon on the Mount. He promises a better world, the fulfillment of the kingdom of God, if we promise to live our lives in the proper spirit.

It was fun the last couple of months to watch with anticipation as President Clinton picked his cabinet members. It was amazing to see how people would drop everything from their former lives in an instant, rush off to Arkansas to be with the president, and to begin a totally new existence as his advisor and servant. It's like Jesus, in today's gospel, picking his twelve apostles. They willingly give up their former lives as fishermen. They throw down their nets, and decide to change their lives completely, so that they can follow and serve their friend and savior, Jesus Christ.

The difference is that the cabinet members need to be above reproach—their past can come back to haunt them just as the sun comes back to Barrow, Alaska. The confirmation hearings this week were cruel as the criteria for selection are very strict. It seems we as a nation could be a little more like Jesus. He is not quite as severe when he picks his apostles. Anyone can be acceptable to God. He knows these men's hearts. He is aware of their weaknesses and sins. But he is forgiving. All he cares about is the present. They express willingness to change their hearts, to follow him, and to serve him.

Jesus offers the same invitation to us that he offered to his apostles. He asks us to give up the sins of our past and to join his cause for justice, love, and peace. He asks us to follow him with renewed enthusiasm, to help change the world for the better, and make God's kingdom flourish on this earth—so that people in darkness may see his light again.

As followers of Christ, we are called to be bearers of his light. Christ's light has come into the world. It is up to us to make sure that the light of his love and compassion shines in the darkness and gloom of the modern world. As Christians, we can let a little light shine by being people who care for others in our prayer, our words, and in our actions.

This weekend Chris and Wendy Dols are going to have their baby Bria baptized in our parish. Bria's life will become as a burning candle, helping Christ's light to shine in this world. When we were baptized, Christ enkindled his light in each one of us as well. I'd like to close by reciting the prayer that the priest offered on your behalf at the time your godparents lit your baptismal candle: "Receive the light of Christ. This light is entrusted to you to be kept burning brightly. You have been enlightened by Christ. You are to walk always as a child of the light. Keep the flame of faith alive in your heart. And when the Lord comes, may you go out to meet him in the company of all the Saints." We make this prayer through Jesus Christ our Lord. Amen.

Delivered at the Church of St. John in Grand Marais
on the Third Sunday of the Church Year
January 24, 1993

The Super Bowl and the Beatitudes

As the Super Bowl approaches, some images begin to creep into my mind: domination, joy of victory, civilized war between cities, no mercy, grudge matches, power, bragging rights, macho men, golden rings, million-dollar contracts, the agony of defeat, and the shame and humiliation of being vanquished. About the only things that the Super Bowl has to do with the beatitudes is a single-hearted team spirit, and a willingness to suffer for what you believe in!

Jesus Christ sees the world a bit differently from the way most of us do. What is important to us is usually a stumbling block to true spirituality. In other words, most human beings do not really know what is good for them. For Christ, the greatest victories come from defeat. The Vikings and the Broncos should feel proud to have lost four Super Bowls each. Power comes from weakness. Untold riches come from poverty of spirit.

Part of the homily delivered at the Church of St. John in Grand Marais
on the Fourth Sunday of the Church Year
January 31, 1993

Our Brilliant Little Light

Last summer I was in Nevada touring Lehman's Cave in Great Basin National Park. At the beginning of the tour, our guide gave us each a flashlight to help light the way. That flashlight was the most important thing in my life for the next hour and a half. I would have been totally lost and helpless without it. At one point on the tour, we entered a huge room with great formations all over. And the guide told us to all switch our lights off at the same time. We found ourselves in total darkness. It was an amazing phenomenon. It wasn't like turning the bedroom lights off at night. There was no city light. No stars, no refracted atmospheric light. There was nothingness. There was a feeling inside of complete emptiness. Although the room was full of people, I felt entirely alone. I also felt helpless and terrified; I did not know where to turn; I was afraid to take a single step in any direction lest I stumble on a rock or bump into someone. Perhaps that is what it's like for a child to lose a parent through death or divorce.

The guide told us that if we had to stand there forever in the dark, our eyes would never adjust to the lack of light. We would never see a thing again. It made me think about what a wonderful gift the human eye is, and how blessed we are to be able to see the world in which we walk.

Not all of us have that precious gift of sight. I was on retreat with my fellow priests all last week in Buffalo, Minnesota, and our retreat master was totally blind in both eyes. Every once in a while he would bump into the podium and say: "Who put that there!" A couple of times he stumbled into chairs. He had a Bible written in Braille from which he read to us. We had fun playing cribbage with him using a deck of Braille cards. But we still had to state the rank and suit of each card as we played it so that he had a sense of the play. Because of his great memory, we only had to tell him once.

He heard you tell him your name once, and he remembered you for the rest of the week just by the sound of your voice. Incredible.

We all took turns being his guide, leading him to his room, lunch, or mass. It gave us all a chance to be a light in his life. To show him the way, to guide him through the cave of his darkness, as though we were his flashlights. But, he was much more a light to us than we were to him. He was a man full of great spiritual insight. Even though no daylight came into him from the outside, you could tell that the spirit of Jesus Christ had illuminated him from within. And he had learned to let that light shine very well in his life. He was truly an inspiration to all the priests.

Jesus Christ came into this world as a light shining in the darkness to guide us, to illuminate our minds, to brighten our hearts, to share God's infinite life and love with us.

Today he calls us the light of the world. We are his Easter candles, providing the wicks for Christ to bring his light and love to all people. We need to let that light shine. Today the Scriptures tell us not only to be light, they tell us how to do it: "Share your bread with the hungry, shelter the oppressed and the homeless, clothe the naked when you see them, then your light shall break forth like the dawn." "If you remove from your midst oppression, false accusation, and malicious speech, if you bestow your bread on the hungry, and satisfy the afflicted, then light shall rise for you in the darkness, and your gloom shall become as bright as the sun shining at noon. The just man is a light in darkness—he lavishly gives to the poor."

Our retreat master was a sign to us that no one is whole or perfect; we don't need to be. Our spiritual and physical handicaps need not keep us from being Christ's candles that help light up the world. All Jesus needs is our cooperation, our willingness to help share his light. He can take what little we have to offer and make it seem brilliant. That is Paul's point today:

> As for myself, brothers and sisters, I did not come proclaiming God's testimony with any great eloquence or wisdom. When I came among you, it was in weakness and fear, and with much trepidation. My message and my preaching had none of the persuasive force of wise argumentation, but the convincing power of the Spirit.

You don't know how comforting those words are for a priest to hear. My salvation doesn't depend on how well I preach. I do the best I can and let God do his work. That reading is an invitation for me to relax and let the spirit fill my heart, and not worry too much about whether I am accomplishing any good. Christ will do his own good, if I just offer him my heart.

That's true for each one of us as well. We don't have to be perfect lovers. We all make mistakes and have personality flaws that may never change. But, big deal. God understands. He made us imperfect. The nice thing is that Christ is infinitely patient and forgiving. He can use us no matter what our limitations are. Let's let him come into our hearts this morning and allow his spirit to fill us with his light. Just think what a bright existence humanity could have if we all let Christ light our candles to share his light with the world.

Delivered at the Church of St. John in Grand Marais
on the Fifth Sunday of the Church Year
February 7, 1993

We Should Not Be Ashamed of Temptation

Happy Valentine's Day. We are all brothers and sisters in Christ, and I love you all. I'd like to begin today by telling you a little joke that our retreat master told us a few days ago. I thought it was funny, and it seems appropriate for this holiday.

The National Federation of Priests Council was having its annual convention in Dallas, and the theme was "There Are No Problems—Just Opportunities." Big signs all over advised: "There Are No Problems—Just Opportunities." One of the priests looked a little worried. He stumbled up to the reception desk, and said to the clerk: "Sir, I have a big problem." The clerk replied, "Father, read the signs: There are no problems—just opportunities." The priest said: "Call it what you will, but there is a woman in my room."

So, the clerk was right. The priest had an opportunity, to either satisfy his lust, or to be a man of strong moral fiber and resist temptation. Lust is an exciting word, isn't it? It can be used as a noun or a verb; but, either way, it is still an action word: just to hear it makes our adrenaline start pumping. I guess Valentine's Day is as good as any to discuss it.

Like the priest in the joke, we all have many opportunities in life, plenty of opportunities to do good and to do bad. In today's gospel, Jesus is discussing those opportunities to do bad. Traditionally, we have referred to them as near occasions of sin. Moments of temptation. Deliberately placing ourselves or accidentally finding ourselves in environments which stimulate us to a point where we lose control of our basic desires and strong emotions. We should not be ashamed of temptation. As the Bible says, "Jesus was tempted in every way that we are, but he did not sin." It may seem like Jesus is telling us that lust and anger are sinful feelings. I don't believe that is really what he is saying. Lust and anger are very positive gifts to us from God, as is each body part. But what we do with them is another matter. Our bodies and feelings can be very sinful if used in the wrong way.

God gave us our tongues so that we could communicate with one another, to speak words of love, to work out difficult problems, to tell others what we are feeling inside, to share information, to discipline and to teach. But we can also use our tongues to lie, cheat, slander, gossip, utter terroristic threats, or speak words that do much more damage than would hurling sticks and stones. God gave us our hands to assist our fellow human beings, help us make a living, create beautiful works of art, caress the special people whom we love, and hold the hand of a little child. But we can also use them to steal from others, form a fist and beat somebody up, pull the trigger on a gun, wield a sword, or push a button that could destroy the world.

In the same way our sexual organs are not evil. They are gifts to us from God as are our sexual feelings that deepen our pleasure and our ability to love and help God create life. They help us to take an interest in others, instead of just living for ourselves. They help us to form community, to share intimacy, and get so deeply interested in another person that we want to spend the rest of our lives with them. Sexual feelings help sustain a permanent commitment to each other so that we can create children and provide an atmosphere of undying and everlasting love in which to raise them.

But just like with our tongues and with our hands, our lust can be used in evil ways, as well. It can cause us to engage in premarital sex or, even worse, in date rape. It can cause us to go outside of our marriage relationship to satisfy our needs through adultery. It can cause priests to go against our vows of celibacy or, even worse, to engage in acts of pedophilia. And it can turn some otherwise nice people into human monsters who exploit their fellow human beings as mere physical objects to satisfy their bizarre impulses; this in turn causes them to perpetrate some of the most horrendous acts imaginable upon their fellow human beings.

Clearly, it is essential to place some limits on these drives if we want to live a healthy life. The same is true of anger. There is nothing wrong with anger. It is a good thing. Jesus got angry with his disciples when they fought over who of them was the most important. He got upset with the Scribes and the Pharisees when they were more interested in observing the letter of the law as opposed to allowing it to affect their hearts. He even got physically upset when he chased the merchants out of the temple.

Our anger is as much a gift to us from God as is our lust. Anger can help us work out important issues that we might otherwise let go of and forget about. Anger can be a good gauge to help us know what things are really important to us in our lives. Anger can spur us to action, to help Christ work for justice in the world. Anger can help us to communicate important things to those we love. But, again, anger can be a source of evil if it is unchecked. It can turn into a consuming rage and keep us from forgiveness. It can tie us in knots and make us behave in ways that we are ashamed of. Not only can a word spoken in anger hurt deeply, but it can't be taken back; it can only be forgiven. Anger can make us commit acts of violence against others or their property. It can lead us to spouse and child abuse.

For some, lust and anger can be terrible addictions that enslave their lives. If this is true in your case, you probably need some form of professional counseling, which is nothing to be ashamed of. There are great programs available to help you. Give me a call and I can set you up with someone.

Some of us have bouts, or occasional outbursts. We have to trust in God's patience and forgiveness, relying on the forgiveness of our loved ones whom we often hurt unintentionally. Some seem to handle these things well. Mary and the saints might be our examples. We need to look to them with admiration and inspiration and allow them to help transform our lives.

It's good to consider the context in which Jesus' words today are given. They are part of his Sermon on the Mount. He is speaking of the wonderful life that is waiting for us to be lived in God's kingdom. This is a new world order of peace and justice for every person on earth. Today he's asking us to dream big dreams, to think special thoughts that come from God's wisdom, to allow the Holy Spirit to transform the way we think about things, to look at things the way God sees them.

Wouldn't it be nice to have a world where we were interested in others for more than just their bodies? That sounds kind of cynical. Of course we are interested in much more than that. But, it would be so liberating for us to be in a world where it isn't even a consideration.

And wouldn't it be nice to exist in a kingdom free from violence and hate? Where we could all relate to each other in a spirit of total forgiveness with infinite patience and peace. That is a vision that God wants each of us to have. Jesus is telling us that we can begin to work toward that ideal right now. It may not come until we are all in heaven.

But we can at least do our little bit to help. Of course, we will sometimes fail. But we know that our God forgives when we don't live up to the promise of the kingdom.

If you are overcome by hatred, bitterness, anger, or lust, it's time to start praying for miracles in your life. Jesus Christ is the savior of the world. He can save us from our own drives when they get too powerful for us. We need to place our total trust in his life-saving love.

Delivered at the Church of St. John in Grand Marais
on the Sixth Sunday of the Church Year
February 14, 1993

Let 'Em Have Another Whack!
Not an Easy Thing to Do!

Last week, a few of us went to see the movie *Scent of a Woman*. It is a great movie—in my book, the best movie of the year! I think you should all see it if you can put up with the language. I'm not going to give any of the plot away. I don't want to spoil it for you. But there is one climactic scene where the two main characters get into a huge argument that elicits strong emotions from the audience. Well, the scene was obviously too much for a couple of viewers to handle. They got into a loud argument that developed along lines similar to the movie. They distracted the entire audience.

I was fuming inside. These guys were destroying my enjoyment of the film and I wanted to lash out at them. Finally, a heroic fellow got up, walked over to them, spoke calmly to them, quieted them down, and diffused the whole situation. We were all grateful to him. But I, for one, felt guilty and ashamed. I was angry at them and wanted revenge. But this guy took time to care about their needs and helped them to resolve their conflict. Which was the real Christian response to the situation? The answer is fairly obvious in light of to-day's readings: "Are you not aware that you are a temple of God, and that the Holy Spirit dwells in you?" The words of St. Paul cause us to reflect on how sacred each human life is, especially in God's eyes. No wonder God demands that we love one another and that we treat each other with respect.

In the first reading, the Lord says to Moses, "Tell the people, 'Love your neighbor as yourself, and carry no grudges.'" The "no grudges" part is the more difficult. We humans seem to like to hold grudges against other people, even against ourselves. We get hurt by someone, and we want to get even. We like the sound of revenge. The old law says, "An eye for an eye." That's something we can all understand. We can't wait to get back at Toronto and Oakland next summer.

But then Jesus comes along and changes the law. Not only do we have to forgive and not carry grudges, we have to turn our other cheek, and let the guy have another whack at us—not an easy thing to do. Even worse, we have to love our enemies and pray for those who persecute us. When I read this gospel, the first people I always think of are Martin Luther King, Jr., and Mohandas Gandhi, two men who really lived by these principles. They were men whose people were unjustly and brutally treated, but who taught them to work for justice through non-violence. These men ultimately gave up their lives in sacrifice. They did not lift a finger against the people who wronged them. Martin Luther King, Jr., once said, "We must, in strength and humility, learn to meet hate with love."

In the movie *Gandhi*, there is a great scene that is hard to forget. Early in the film, Gandhi and a Christian minister are walking through the streets of a town in South Africa discussing the terrible injustices that existed there among races.

Speaking as a Hindu to the Christian clergyman, Gandhi says, "Does not your New Testament say, 'If your enemy strikes you on the right cheek, offer him the left as well?' " The minister replies, "I think the phrase is used metaphorically. I don't think anyone really takes it seriously." With that, Gandhi offers a beautiful insight:

> I have thought about it a great deal, and I suspect that he meant that you must show courage. Be willing to take a blow—several blows—to show that you will not strike back, nor will you be turned aside. And when you do that, it calls on something in human nature—something that makes your enemy's hatred for you decrease, and his respect increase. Christ grasped that and I have seen it work.

Well, of course, Gandhi was absolutely right, and the movie goes on to show that he not only spoke those words, he lived them throughout the course of his entire life, even though it meant a great deal of personal suffering and, ultimately, his assassination.

Can you imagine the amount of restraint and self-sacrifice one would need to adopt such an outlook on life? In addition to the courage and patience, just think of how much forgiveness a person would need to turn the other cheek. But that is exactly what Jesus demands of us in today's gospel. Love your enemies; pray for those who persecute you. His disciples must be like God when it comes to forgiveness, the God of forgiveness who we meet in the responsorial psalm today:

The Lord is kind and merciful. He pardons all your iniquities, he heals all your ills. He redeems your life from destruction. He crowns you with kindness and compassion. Merciful and gracious is the Lord, slow to anger and abounding in kindness. Not according to our sins does he deal with us, nor does he requite us according to our crimes. The Lord is kind and merciful.

Jesus tells us to forgive others seventy times seven times. He teaches us to pray for the spirit of forgiveness in the Lord's prayer: "Forgive us our trespasses, as we forgive those who trespass against us."

Literature and real life are full of important examples of people weighed down by grudges, people wasting away their lives in hate, and finally discovering how the ability to forgive can free them from torment and return them to a healthy existence. The character of Ben Hur comes to mind. He assumes an obsessive, consuming hatred of Messalah for destroying the lives of his mother and sister. Ironically, it is Ben Hur's own hatred that has destroyed his own life, making him incapable of love. At the end of the movie, Christ works some miracles from the cross, and cures the mother and sister of their leprosy. But the real miracle occurs when the sword is lifted from Ben Hur's own heart, and he is able to forgive and begin to live a genuine life again.

I was touched last week by the story of Gregory K., the little boy from Florida who divorced his real father and mother. His court-appointed father adopted him because he saw parallels from his own life. Both had fathers who were abusive alcoholics. The new dad remembered how hard it was to forgive his own father. He wanted to give the kid an environment in which he could learn to forgive his father too.

After the kid won his case, he was with his new dad by a lake skipping stones. The kid screamed at the top of his lungs, "It's over. I can live again. I hate my father. I never want to see him again." His new dad challenged him on the spot by saying, "One of the reasons I adopted you is because I didn't want you to go through what I went through. I wasted half my life hating my father. The only way I could be truly free was to learn to forgive him. I hope you will start working on forgiving your father, too!"

The kid's response was, "Maybe sometime, but not today." The movie ended right there. But with his new dad, Gregory might be able to learn how to forgive. When we have trouble forgiving, we have to learn how to do it from somebody else such as our own fathers, and especially our father in heaven. That's why prayer and reflection is so important. Sure, we have basic instincts for revenge and grudge-carrying, but we don't have to submit to them. By reflection on our basic instincts, we can analyze the origins of our base instincts, and transform them.

We can allow them to give us more understanding. It all starts with an awareness of our own imperfection. When I read the last line of today's gospel, I bet there was some sadness in our hearts. In a word, "you must be perfected as your heavenly father is perfect." We all know that is impossible for us. But we have a God who loves us anyway, who is definitely forgiving. Just look at the events we are about to celebrate through Lent, Holy Week, and Easter. Jesus Christ is the ultimate example of what a loving, forgiving human being should be like.

We humans—every one of us—are sinful. None of us deserves God's love. Yet Christ came among us with total love. He gave everything he had for us out of love, including his life. The people he loved responded by laughing at him. They told him that nothing good had ever come out of Nazareth. They threw stones at him. When he needed his friends, they betrayed and deserted him. They denied they ever knew him. He was then whipped, beaten, crowned with thorns. He was finally crucified and killed. Even on the cross, he could forgive: "Forgive them, Father—for they do not know what they are doing."

Jesus wasn't just forgiving them from the cross; he was loving the soldiers with all his heart at the exact moment that they were slowly killing him. When he rose from the dead, he did not run off and leave his friends. He went right back among the apostles who abandoned him. And his first words to them were, "Peace be with you!"

He made his deserter, Peter, the foundation of his new church. He took Paul, who was killing his followers, and made him the great saint who spread the gospel throughout the entire Mediterranean. It is important that we reflect on these events in prayer. Is there any reason why we should not forgive our neighbor when we see how much Christ has done for us? There is no reason!

It is our responsibility as Christians to share with others what God has shared with us. And the most important thing he has shared with us is probably his forgiveness.

The true sign that we are Christ's disciples is probably not so much our desire to love as it is our desire to forgive. As Jesus says in the Gospel, "your ability to forgive will prove that you are sons and daughters of your heavenly Father."

What struck me about this year's election was, after all the bitter rivalry and cruel mud-slinging, how gracious George Bush was in defeat and how conciliatory he was in his last days as he left the White House. Nowhere else but in America is something like that possible. We should let that be an example and inspiration to us when we are defeated by others in our own lives. Let go of the past. Forgive those who injure us. Live life anew in the fresh spirit that Jesus demonstrated when he rose from the dead and spoke to his deserters, "my peace I give to you!"

Delivered at the Church of St. John in Grand Marais
on the Seventh Sunday of the Church Year
February 21, 1993

The Paschal Mystery

*Every Christian finds his own special place
in the mysteries of the life of Christ.*

> *Diary of a Country Priest*
> George Bernanos

No More Fear

"Unless the grain of wheat falls to the earth and dies, it remains just a grain; but if it dies it produces much fruit."

There is the story of a priest in Georgia who was called out to an old plantation to bring communion to a one hundred-year-old woman. He got to the door of the gigantic mansion and banged the heavy knocker against it. He waited for about ten minutes, but there was no answer. He pushed open the door a little bit and heard this feeble, little voice say, "Come in! Come in!" So he stepped inside, and found himself standing in a spacious room. Again he heard the voice calling from the other end of a long corridor, "Come in! Come in!"

He opened the door, walked inside, looked around the room, and saw a huge Doberman Pinscher sitting on a carpet in the corner. All of a sudden the dog let out a ferocious growl, leaped into the air, charged the priest, knocked him over, pinned him against the wall with paws on his chest, glistening, sharp teeth at his throat, tongue hanging out onto the priest's neck. The priest, in a state of sheer terror, looked directly into the dog's gleaming eyes, and prayed, "Lord, save me!"

To his surprise, the dog backed off, walked backed to his rug, turned around, and faced the priest. "Well," he thought to himself, "a typical day in the life of a priest!" He uttered a sigh of relief, stood up, brushed off his clothes, and looked around the room again. This time he saw in the other corner a bird cage perched on a stand with a parrot in it saying, "Come in! Come in!"

Well, needless to say, the priest was furious. He shouted out, "Shut up, you lousy bird! Are those the only stinking words you know?"

There was a moment of dead silence, except for the sound of the panting dog. Then the bird began to squawk again, "Attack and kill! Attack and kill!"

That bird in the cage kind of reminds me of God: he is constantly calling us. If we respond to his call, we have no idea of what lies beyond the door. Sometimes it can be pretty dangerous there.

St. Peter accepted God's invitation to follow Christ and ended up getting crucified upside down. St. Paul accepted God's invitation and ended up getting his head cut off for all his efforts. Mary said yes to God's call and was forced to stand and watch as her only son was horribly tortured and killed. And look at Jesus Christ himself. He was the son of God, his dearly beloved. He prayed in the garden, and look what happened to him!

Earlier today, we brought out a beautiful symbol of Jesus Christ— this candle. Christ is the light of the world. He brightens up our hearts and brings joy to our lives. But this didn't just happen. He had to put out an awful lot just to become our light.

The cross is another great symbol of Jesus Christ, a symbol of his great sacrifice, of his total giving for us. It reminds us of the little sacrifices that we have to make in our lives to get what we want.

If we want to be good athletes, we have to work out and practice until it hurts. If we want good grades, we have to give up some fun now and then to study. If we want to improve our spiritual lives, it means sacrifice too, such as giving up a weekend to attend a retreat like this. And we discover that sacrifice leads to great rewards. But none of those little sacrifices compares to the suffering and death that Jesus endured out of love for us.

As a kid in school, I used to feel so sad when I saw Jesus on the cross. What a terrible death, I thought! But, now, when I look at the cross, it makes me feel happy inside. It makes me have an overflowing love in my heart to think that Jesus would go through all of that because he loves me, and he loves you. He proved his own words. He said, "No greater love has a person than this, that he lays down his life for his friends!"

I have a question for you! If the death of Jesus was so awful, why do they call it "Good Friday"? Because he freed the world from sin! Because Jesus put God's will above his own! Because he died out of love for us!

How many of you have seen the movie *Prince of Tides*? I love that final scene in the movie where Nick Nolte is driving across the bridge and he reflects on the special woman-psychiatrist in his life who liberated him from the demons that haunted him from the past and imprisoned his present. She cured him and gave him the free-

dom to live again. As he reaches the crest of the bridge, he spontane-
ously feels a surge of love and welling up inside and blurts out her
name from the depths of his heart, "Lowenstein! Lowenstein!"

I have a love like that in my life, too! Sometimes when I am
driving along in my car, I find myself speaking the name out loud,
"Jesus Christ, Jesus Christ, I love you!" I look at this cross, and
I see the man who willingly died for me out of love. A feeling of gratitude overwhelms me when I think that he suffered all of this for me.
His death has liberated me from my sins. And I am free to live again
because of his sacrifice!

Do you remember the movie a few years back that caused such
a stink? It was called *The Last Temptation of Christ*. Thousands of people
picketed the movie without having seen it because they thought it was
an insult to the Christian faith to portray Jesus as having sexual desires
just like the rest of us. They should have watched the movie before
they objected to it.

I think it is perhaps one of the top ten movies ever made. It is
certainly the best movie ever made about Jesus Christ. Towards the
end of the movie, Jesus is in the garden. He is actually sweating blood.
He doesn't want to die. He loves life. He had just a few days earlier
raised his friend Lazarus from the dead. He prays, "God, don't let
this happen to me. I don't want to be crucified. I don't want to suffer. I certainly don't want to die. I want to live!" But he goes to his
crucifixion anyway with a look of despair on his face.

As he is hanging on the cross, the devil comes along disguised
as an angel and tempts him into coming down off the cross so that
he might experience all the great things he will be missing if he gives
up his life. But, as he is going through the last temptation, something wonderful happens—a transformation takes place in his attitude: he comes to see God's plan and why he must die for the sake
of the redemption of the world.

Then he climbs back up on the cross and, as he is suffering there,
turns his eyes to heaven, smiles at God, and shouts out in a loud voice,
"I want to be crucified; I really do want to be crucified." And then
he dies with a look of perfect peace on his face.

We remember his willingness to die every time we celebrate mass
together. In the second Eucharistic Prayer, we recite these words,
"Before he was given up to death, a death he freely accepted, he took
bread and gave you thanks!" Jesus Christ was happy to die for our
sins.

The point I want to make today is that death is not evil. It is the ultimate way to get to God. When we die on this earth, we can look forward to new life with God in heaven. Don't get me wrong, I am not advocating suicide. He loves life just as much as we do. After all, that's why he created us. And that's why he hates abortion and suicide so much. He wants us to live our lives to the full. But, my point is that we must all die some day. We don't have to be afraid of that death.

I used to be afraid of death. But not any more. I have recently discovered that I have a form of cancer for which there is no known treatment. I am going to die in a few years. But, whatever I suffer in this life is not so bad. I know it is only temporary. I know that I can look forward to something really great that lies just beyond it. An eternal life of light, happiness and peace in God's heavenly kingdom.

Most people are not in the situation I am in. People like yourselves expect to live quite a long life yet. But, there are other ways to look at death. Christ calls each one of us to die in little ways every day. These little deaths help us grow stronger in our Christian faith.

Over the next few weeks of Lent, especially Holy Week, we are going to be celebrating both death and resurrection. Jesus is not the only one who died and rose again! We all die and rise every day in little ways, and sometimes in very big ways. It seems God uses this process of death and resurrection in all of creation. When it happens to us, we need to have the faith to trust that it is all part of God's plan for us.

A caterpillar buries itself in an ugly cocoon only to emerge later as a beautiful butterfly. The leaves die and fall to the earth in autumn so that new life may bud forth with the coming spring. After the storm comes a beautiful rainbow. After a hurricane or an earthquake, people join together as brothers and sisters to build a better world. After the eruption of a destructive volcano comes new earth, fertile soil, and a new kind of spectacular beauty. After a long winter, we can really appreciate beautiful days like this one. After sin comes a wonderful experience of God's forgiveness. And all of this gets us ready for the big one! After our death on earth comes eternal life with God in heaven.

I have met some people who think that suffering is evil and joy is good. Where would I be in my faith if I thought that my cancer was evil? Even in my sickness, I have a strong faith that God loves me infinitely. Both joy and sorrow are part of God's world. Suffering is good. Would it shock you if I said that suffering is as much a gift to us from God as any joy or happiness? Well, you can count on it as absolute fact!

From the people I have seen, anyway, suffering is what really forges the strongest kind of faith in their lives. With positive experiences all the time, our faith would be very weak and superficial and we would be like spoiled little brats. Suffering gives us strength and endurance to face the real challenges of life. It teaches us what true commitment is all about. It helps us to recognize our need for God's salvation in our lives. And it enables us to identify with and appreciate what Christ went through for us on the cross. In a word, suffering goes a long way to help make us holy.

You want to hear a mind-boggling quote from St. Paul? This is what he says in his Letter to the Corinthians, "The message of the cross is complete absurdity to those who have no faith; but, to us who are experiencing salvation, it is the very power of God."

Faith in Jesus Christ's death and resurrection can be a difficult struggle and it takes courage and a big risk to take that leap of faith. If you work at it and try to say, "I believe that you died for me, Lord, and I believe that you are still alive in me today," then your life can be enriched with new and profound meaning. We can find something good coming out of the most horrible situations in life. It means that we can forgive others in the hope that a dead relationship can be restored. It means that just when we thought our faith was dead, or when we thought that our spiritual life was dried up, we can expect to meet Christ on the road. It means that our loved ones who have died are not gone forever. We will meet them someday again in heaven.

I'd like to mention a few guys from the past who really believed in this process of death and resurrection, who followed Christ's example and gave up their lives for the sake of Christianity. One of my favorite martyrs is Ignatius of Antioch. He was captured by the Romans and was being carted off to Rome to be fed to the lions in the Coliseum. He wrote a letter in which he goes into grotesque detail, so you may want to cover your ears if you don't like horror tales. As Ignatius put it way back in about the year one hundred A.D.,

> I am corresponding with all the churches and bidding them all realize that I am voluntarily dying for God. I will be fodder for wild beasts.

That is how I can get to God. I am God's wheat and I am being ground
by the teeth of wild beasts to make a pure loaf for Christ. Come fire,
cross, battling with wild beasts, wrenching of bones, mangling of limbs,
crushing of my whole body, cruel tortures of all sorts, only let me get
to Jesus Christ! Not the wide bounds of earth nor the kingdoms of
this world will avail me anything. I would rather die and get to Christ
than reign over the ends of the earth. By suffering and death, I shall
be emancipated by Jesus Christ, and united to him, I shall rise to
freedom.

Inspiring stuff, eh? You see Ignatius's profound faith in God,
and his hope for future glory. He does not view martyrdom as tragedy
or defeat, but as victory and glorification. To me, for a person who
has cancer, I find those words quite inspiring. They give me the courage to look beyond death to something greater that lies ahead.

Another example of men willing to die for Christ were the first
Jesuit priests in the sixteen hundreds who brought Christianity to the
Iroquois of New York—a people who weren't too receptive to the
message. Fr. Isaac Jogues was captured by the Mohawks and forced
to run the gauntlet, after which they took clam shells and cut off his
fingers. He escaped, returned to Rome, and had to get special permission from the pope to offer mass without his fingers. Then you
know what he did? He went right back among the same people to
try again. He and six other priests were captured, tortured, and killed
for their faith.

It reminds me of some modern day Jesuit priests. Do you remember in El Salvador a few years back at which time a death squad mur-
dered seven Jesuits in their rectory? You know what the astounding
thing about that incident was? Immediately afterward, the Jesuits had
ten priests who came forward and volunteered to go to El Salvador
to take their places. I am reminded of the movie, *The Mission,* wherein
a Jesuit goes to Brazil to work among the natives. They crucify him
on a cross and push him over a three hundred-foot-high waterfall.
In the very next scene another Jesuit priest climbs the waterfall to
take his place.

What gives these guys the courage to sacrifice their lives this way?
The secret is their deep faith, their conviction that they are doing
Christ's work to help save the world, and their firm belief in the resur-
rection.

This is probably very disrespectful to say, but I sometimes think
that it would be much easier to die as a martyr than to continue liv-

ing as a Christian. One moment of terrible suffering and then it is over, with only an eternal happiness in heaven to follow.

The rest of us have a very slow, sometimes painful, Christian death. By our little sacrifices and sufferings every day that we endure for the kingdom, we discover that our faith is not always the easiest thing in the world to live with. I've been talking quite a bit about physical death, but there is another kind of death. I use the word death in a figurative way. You sometimes hear the expression "dying to ourselves." That means we make little sacrifices to come closer to Christ or to help our family or community grow in love.

We are often tempted to live very selfish lives. To look out for number one and not be concerned about others. When I die to myself, I attempt to put other people first. Or it means that I am going to exchange something immediate for a better life later. There are many ways we can die to ourselves, the first of which is socially. Two virtues that help here are obedience and love.

We live in a free country. But that doesn't mean we can do anything we want. We have to give up some of our freedom, obeying our laws out of respect for each other. We die to ourselves by being obedient to our parents so that things go better at home. We die to ourselves by being obedient in school so that we can create a better atmosphere in which to learn.

Another way to die socially is to sacrifice for the good of others. Here, in a newspaper account, is an example of some people who really died to themselves for somebody else, and it also shows how even better things come out of a situation if we sacrifice for others:

The high school senior class in a small town in Connecticut had been saving their money for a trip to Washington. The fund grew larger and larger, and the day of the trip was coming closer and closer. The students were getting more and more excited about the trip to our nation's capital. Suddenly, they learned that a classmate had cancer. The treatment would be costly. The young people voted to turn over their travel fund to help with their classmate's expenses, though it meant giving up the trip.

Word of their actions got around fast. A flood of donations poured in from all sides so that the class was able to realize their dream after all. All thirty-three of them, including the stricken student, made the trip to Washington where they were honored in many special ways, including a personal visit to see the president.

That shows the great things that can happen when people are ready to die to themselves for the sake of others.

A spirit of sacrifice never gets old. It is the one thing that never fails to inspire us. Seeing one person or a group of people sacrifice for others always seems to enrich us in the depths of our hearts. It makes us want to do the same thing.

A second way to die to ourselves is spiritually. Here we need to work at the virtue of humility. Christ said in the beatitudes, "Blessed are the poor in spirit. Theirs is the kingdom of God."

Mary had the humility to say to the angel, "Let it be done to me according to your word." Jesus had the humility to pray in the garden, "your will, not mine, be done, Father."

And we need the humility to die to our own self-importance and put God first in our lives. If we are ever going to experience God's salvation in our lives, we must first have the humility to admit that we need a savior. All the saving love and activity of Jesus Christ in the word isn't going to help us one bit if we don't have enough humility to say, "Lord, I can't make it on my own. I need your help! Only you can be my savior!"

But, we get too caught up in our own self-importance. We are too proud to rely on another for help. "I don't need God. I can work out my own problems. I can save myself!"

A lot of times our whole modern world seems to say that everything revolves around ourselves. We have to take ourselves out of the center and put Christ there instead. I like to use the analogy of our solar system. All intelligent life exists on earth, but earth is still not the center of things. The sun is the center. Everything else revolves around it as it gives off light, warmth, and sustains our lives.

In the same way, we need the humility to say that we are not the center or our own existence. We need God. The gift of his salvation. As Christians, the son of God must be our center. Our lives must revolve around his spirit. He is the Son who lights up our lives, gives warmth in the darkness of winter, and sustains us with his everlasting life.

I've worked on a number of TEC weekends and the kids have a saying, "Let go, and let God!" It means to put our lives in his hands, and to rely on him. That takes a lot of humility, and that is one important way to die to ourselves.

One final kind of death is psychological death. We need to let go of some of the things that are keeping us from being authentic human beings. For me, that means letting go of my shyness. It takes a lot of energy for me to give a talk like this in an unfamiliar parish because I have to work at coming out of myself a little bit and making an effort to meet new people. That's hard for me, but I always find it worthwhile and rewarding.

Part of psychological death is the act of forgiveness—learning to forgive others, and learning to forgive ourselves when we are not perfect. When Jesus was hanging on the cross, he prayed, "forgive them, Father, for they do not know what they are doing." We need to take a lesson from him and learn how to forgive.

We experience death and resurrection in community in the act of forgiving each other. I'm sure you've experienced this at home. There are times when we get on each other's nerves. We hurt the people we love the most. We sin against each other. Things can get pretty miserable. The atmosphere in the home can become a state of living death.

But what happens to a family when people start to die to themselves? When one person says, "I'm sorry!" or, "I forgive you! You hurt me deeply but I still love you!" A reconciliation has begun. A transformation takes place in your home. An atmosphere of suspicion and hate is changed into one of love and trust. It's fun to be part of a loving family again. An environment of death becomes an environment of new life. But it takes dying to ourselves, and the ability to allow God to raise us up.

In the movie *Little Big Man* the wise old Indian chief tells the story of a brave warrior who had a little body, but a big heart. On the day of battle, he went out in front of his braves and shouted, "It's a great day to die!" His courage inspired his fellow warriors to ride into battle and sacrifice their lives to save the village.

And it is a great day for us to die in the service of Christ. During this talk I have told you about how Christ willingly died for us. And I have told you about how some people have willingly died for Christ. It is our turn to get on the band wagon. To follow Christ's example, to be a suffering servant for our neighbors. To die to ourselves is to live out our baptisms. To be a Christian means to be a man or a woman for others.

I would now like you to relax and close your eyes and take a few moments to reflect on the things to which you must die in your own life to get closer to Christ this Easter. I'd like to close by reciting those special words from the prayer of St. Francis that speak about dying for others:

Prayer of St. Francis

Make me a channel of your peace.
Where there is hatred, let me bring your love.
Where there is injury, your pardon, Lord.
And where there's doubt, true faith in you.

Oh master, grant that I may never seek
So much to be consoled as to console.
To be understood as to understand.
To be loved as to love with all my soul.

Make me a channel of your peace.
Where there's despair in life, let me bring hope.
Where there is darkness, only light,
And where there's sadness, ever joy.

Oh master grant that I may never seek
So much to be consoled as to console.
To be understood as to understand.
To be loved as to love with all my soul.

Make me a channel of your peace.
It is in pardoning that we are pardoned,
In giving of ourselves that we receive,
And in dying that we're born to eternal life.

Delivered to the Teens Encounter Christ Retreatants
February 14, 1992

Ashes, Lent, and Easter

Around your throne
the saints, our brothers and sisters,
sing your praise forever.
Their glory fills us with joy,
and their communion with us in your Church
gives us inspiration and strength
as we hasten on our pilgrimage of faith,
eager to meet them.

Preface of All Saints

Jack Palance's Lenten Lesson

Up here in the north woods, for people who enjoy the cold out-doors, February is a winter wonderland. But for those of us who aren't into winter sports, it's one big wasteland. Lent comes at just the right time of year, if you ask me. Winter can get very long and cold. We long for the spring thaw. Our lives can feel pretty empty.

I think that feeling of emptiness is a great thing, provided we don't try to fill it up with the wrong things. I love the emptiness and loneliness of winter because I know that it is a gift to me from God that gives me a chance to fill my cup with Christ. Lent is that special time when we all make a new effort at developing a spiritual depth to our lives and get to know Christ at a deeper level.

As we will see on Sunday, Jesus Christ spent forty days in the wasteland himself. He needed that time to strengthen his will and overcome temptation. It was a time of hungering and thirsting for food and water as well as thirsting for an obedient relationship with God his Father.

We too begin forty days in the wasteland today on Ash Wednes-day. It is a time for us to hunger and thirst for the Lord as well. We long to have him fill our emptiness with his limitless love.

The summer before last, I saw the movie *City Slickers,* and I really liked the advice that Jack Palance gave to his trail hands: decide what that one thing is that is important to you, and then go live for that one thing. Ever since that time, I have tried to make God the num-ber one thing in my life.

I have pursued his presence with varying degrees of commitment and success. I have faltered and recovered time and again in my rela-tionship with him. Of course, I don't have a family to complicate things. Maybe you folks should have two number one things in your life to go along with Christ's two commandments of love: God and family. It is good for us to hunger and thirst for total union with both of them. But, like me in my relationship with God, it is impossible for any of us to sustain a perfect union. We falter. We have our ups and downs. We need special moments to make a concerted effort at restoration and renewal; we need periods of sacrifice, prayer, special activities, and rituals of love to keep our families going.

Lent is the time for us to recommit ourselves to the family of God, to fast and pray and love in special ways. It is a time to express our sorrow for the past and strive for a better present and future.

This will be a special Lent for our parish. Our thirst as a Catholic parish will be joined by the thirst of some new catechumens who are developing a deeper relationship with Christ. We will welcome Rolph and Layne Linquist and their family into our parish community on the night of the Easter Vigil. We will baptize Sean Doucette. In addition, our confirmation students will be preparing to enter more deeply into God's family.

This year, celebrating the rituals of initiation with our confirmation class and our catechumens will be a great opportunity for all of us to recommit ourselves to God at a deeper level and also to offer a spirit of welcome to our new candidates for baptism and confirmation.

We are about to be marked with the great sign of repentance, the blessed ashes of last year's palm branches, which remind us that we are mortal beings. As we receive the ashes tonight, let them be an outward sign of our inward thirst to be one with our savior.

Delivered at the Church of St. John in Grand Marais on Ash Wednesday February 24, 1993

Thirst and Satisfaction

One day when Cain and Abel were getting along pretty well as brothers, they were out working in the desert in front of their shack. Cain looked down into the valley and said to Abel, "Look at that beautiful, green garden over there. It goes on for miles and miles. Why doesn't our family live there instead of on this barren, burnt-out, God-forsaken wasteland?"

Abel answered, "Don't you remember when we were little kids? We used to live there until Mom and Dad ate us out of house and home!"

Ever since those early days, when Adam and Eve were kicked out of the Garden, we human beings have longed to return to it.

Jesus spent forty days out in the Negev Desert. His stay there was much like our lives on earth. Our existence in this world is similar to the lengthy sojourn of the Israelites who wandered around in the desert for forty years. It's certainly a livable world, but we grumble and long for more, a land flowing with milk and honey. We are fed by God in many ways. But it is not what we want, and it is not enough. We're never satisfied. We thirst for new life in a rich fertile garden somewhere over the rainbow.

The area where Jesus spent his forty days in the desert is in the mountains above the town of Jericho. In fact, from the traditional site of the Mount of Temptation, where the devil led Jesus for his third trial, you can look down over one thousand feet into the arid Jordan River valley. The town of Jericho, below, is a plush, green, fertile, irrigated oasis. It stretches for miles through the hot, barren, dried-up wasteland of the Jordan Valley.

When I was in Israel, a group of us climbed that mountain in the desert heat and looked down on the same beautiful sight that Jesus saw. We were lucky, though. We had canteens along with us. We were able to quench our thirsts and attain some degree of satisfaction and peace.

It must have been awfully tempting for the human Jesus to give up his fast and head down to Jericho to satisfy his hunger and thirst with a variety of green vegetables, juicy fruits, and all the cool, clean, refreshing water he could ever want. But that wasn't in God's plan yet. First, he had to fast and pray in preparation for the journey up to Jerusalem where he would suffer and die on the cross. The course of his path ahead of him was clearly visible: a journey through suffering and death. But he also knew that on the other side was resurrection and glory—a rich, fertile oasis for eternity, a Garden of Eden which God has intended for us all along since the very beginning of our creation.

We, too, know the road that leads to that garden, especially since we have Jesus Christ as a guide to follow. The only trouble is that there are so many temptations along the side of the road trying to lead us off course. It's not an easy road to follow. Like Jesus, we need to spend time in the desert to strengthen our resolve.

Jesus' experience in the desert was just the opposite of my experience last October and November. I had an incredibly voracious appetite and an unquenchable thirst. I was eating like crazy, and no matter how much I ate I was still terribly hungry. I was constantly ingesting a variety of liquids: pop, orange juice, grape juice, Kool-Aid, root beer floats, chocolate malts, plain ice water. But no matter what I did, I could not quench my thirst. I got weaker and weaker and was losing weight at a rapid rate. So after a few weeks of this, I finally got smart and went to see the doctor. He said, "I'm glad you came to see me! You could have continued to eat and drink as much as you wanted, but eventually you would have starved to death. Your body is not absorbing any food."

It turned out that I have diabetes. He said: "So, do you want to die, or do you want to check into the hospital for a few days and get your body regulated? I said, "Can I have a few days to think about it?" I checked in and the results were amazing. All that food and water was doing nothing for me at all, but a few drops of insulin a day was enough to help me get my strength back and live again.

God's love is like that insulin. A little bit goes a long way to help keep us well fed and nourished. The gospel says that we cannot live on bread alone. God can quench our thirst and satisfy our hunger with a few words of Scripture every day. Jesus Christ is the Word of God; he is the insulin our bodies need to help us absorb the nutrients of God's life-sustaining food. Through prayer we get a couple shots a day by acknowledging Christ's presence in our lives. If we turn to him for strength, the rest of our diet starts falling into place.

The problem is that we are tempted along other lines. For diabetics, too much sugar will cause our bodies to waste away. We need self-discipline to watch our diets very carefully. We have to sacrifice some of the luxuries that others take for granted. But it's more than worth it to have a healthy existence.

The same is true of all of us in a spiritual way. The things that often look so sweet and inviting to us will keep us from getting to the garden we so desperately long for. Just like Adam and Eve who were tempted by the serpent to eat that delicious-looking fruit, we are beset by demons of all kinds. Even Jesus was tempted by Satan in the desert. We often hunger and thirst for things that can hurt us and lead us to self-destruction—too much alcohol, illegal drugs, illicit sex, wealth, power, or revenge.

What gives us hope is to see, as in today's gospel, that Jesus was able to overcome temptation. He was a human being like us. So he gives us the motivation to work at perfection in our own lives too. St. Paul says in the second reading that whereas Adam gave in to his cravings and led humanity down the destructive path of darkness, sin, and death, Jesus mastered his desires and led us back to the path of light, goodness, and life.

We all need self-discipline, and that is what this season of Lent is all about. It is about forty days in the desert, to willingly deprive ourselves of unnecessary luxuries. It is a way for us to grow in strength of character, to overcome temptation when it presents its alluring pleasures. Fasting also helps us to dwell on the important things in life that lead to a healthy spiritual existence: prayer, love of family, simplicity, humility, acceptance, patience, peace, faith, forgiveness, and hope. The list of positive, life sustaining virtues is endless; however, achieving them is another thing. They flow from the desert of sacrifice, and lead to the garden of life.

I'd like to close by saying a few words about a wonderful ceremony that we are celebrating today at the beginning of Lent with our confirmation students and those who will be welcomed into the Catholic Church at the Easter Vigil. Talking about Jericho today reminded me of another experience I had out there in the Jordan Desert. A few of us were in Qumran, about ten miles south of Jericho in the desert at the top of the Dead Sea. The buses had stopped running, so we had to walk to Jericho to catch a bus back to Jerusalem. We had the choice of walking through the desert or on the paved road which wound an extra five miles. The desert route looked fairly flat anyway, so we figured we could make it in about three hours or so. We were mistaken. It took about eight hours. We soon discovered why the road took such a lengthy, winding course.

Our supposedly straight path took us up steep hills, down into ravines and deep canyons, around gigantic rock towers that were unscalable, and through piles of camel dung that stunk to high heaven. The desert was hot and miserable. But the thing that kept us going was the sight of the beautiful green oasis of Jericho that kept getting closer and closer.

As I mentioned earlier, we are on a journey like that. And God provides many oases to help us get to the garden. The sacraments are like some of those times. In baptism we receive the fresh waters of new life. In confirmation we receive the strength of the spirit to continue the journey. We hope our experience takes us closer and closer in the loving relationship with Jesus Christ who refreshes our souls. Today is a day to look ahead of you and envision that beautiful green oasis of confirmation gleaming in the distance. Imagine Christ ahead of you with outstretched arms, waiting to receive you with love and a soothing glass of Kool-Aid.

Today our catechumens and confirmation students will begin their journey in earnest. They will register their names in the Parish Roll Book, and the bishop has invited them all to the Cathedral to celebrate when Lent is over. This is a chance for all of us to renew our commitment to Christ as well, allowing him to quench the thirsts which we so strongly long to have satisfied.

Delivered at the Church of St. John in Grand Marais on the First Sunday of Lent February 28, 1993

A Light to Make All Things Bearable

When I go on vacation, I don't relax the way I should. I get obsessed trying to cram a lifetime into each day. I rarely stop to eat; I rush from one sight to the next. Consequently, I don't take the time to appreciate each spot the way I should.

Last summer, when I was out in Moab, Utah, I drove thirty-five miles out of the way on a spur road to get to Dead Horse State Park so that I could look down on Canyonlands National Park three thousand feet below. I parked the car, jogged up to the lookout, peered over the edge for a second, and ran back to the car. When I sat at the steering wheel to leave, I said to myself, "Mark, you idiot, that is one of the most spectacular sights on earth, and you'll probably never get another chance to see it!"

So, I walked back up to the lookout, and spent forty-five minutes just sitting at the edge of the canyon wall, absorbing its awesome, spectacular beauty. It was a glorious hour. I felt like I was in heaven looking down on the earth far below.

As I was up there, I was praying about my physical condition and I thought to myself, "Mark, the next year is probably going to be a pretty rough one for you. You are going to have to ingrain this sight in your memory so that you can draw on it when you need some extra strength."

Needless to say, I have drawn on that memory and it has given me a lot of support on rough days. I thank God for that blessed last summer.

Jesus and his apostles seem to be in the same situation in the gospel. They had a wonderful experience of the transfiguration on Mount Tabor. Peter loved it so much that he wanted to pitch some tents and stay up there forever. But Jesus seemed to be in a bigger hurry. He knew that they had to return to earth and go to Jerusalem where he would ultimately suffer and die for our salvation.

Peter didn't understand at the time. But, eventually, he suffered and died for Christ in the same way. Though the transfiguration lasted only a moment, that memory probably enriched Peter's life and helped him to make it through some of his tougher times.

In the gospel today, God speaks from heaven these words: "This is my beloved son in whom I am well pleased!" We have heard these words elsewhere in scripture. They are the same words spoken about the suffering servant by Isaiah in his famous poem. We hear them read on Good Friday in the first reading.

Matthew uses those words to signify what God's intention is for Jesus. Christ is to take up his cross and be the servant of his people. The experience of the transfiguration is a temporary respite for Jesus Christ from his terrible burden. Not only was it a brief pause to relax, but it provided a small taste of the glory which was to come after the resurrection: "Do not tell anyone of this vision until the son of man rises from the dead!"

The transfiguration is a sign for each one of us as well. We are to pick up our crosses and follow Christ down the road to crucifixion in which we become "suffering servants in his kingdom."

Without moments of peace in Christ's company, the task becomes unbearable for us. We need to take time to seek out special places of prayer, to sit and relax and be with Christ and allow his presence to transform us. Such moments do five things: they enlighten us at the moment of their occurrence; they refresh us and change the way we look at things; they encourage us to put our faith and trust in the God we cannot see; they stay with us in our memories so that we have something in reserve when the going gets rough, especially in dry periods when we don't have time to take off for prayer; and they give us a better world to come. It's like Abraham in the first reading today who enjoys a special moment in God's presence. God promises great things for him in the future if he will have faith, and if he will journey to an unknown, distant land. That special moment was all he needed. It was like a contract with God, a special event to seal their covenant. He thought back on it many times in his life to give him courage. He also looked forward to the completion of its promise.

Our baptisms are much like that. God calls us to be part of his kingdom. He frees us from sin and promises us joy in a new life to come if we will take the journey with his son. At baptism, we received his light and we should try to carry that light with us in everything we do.

Dr. Henry Jones spent his whole life searching for the Holy Grail that Jesus used to contain his blood at the Last Supper. When Henry finally found the Holy Grail near the end of his life, halfway around the world, in an ancient tomb, in the middle of a forsaken wasteland, he had to let it go forever to save the life of his son.

Indiana Jones asked his father what he got out of the whole experience; and the old man's response was one word: "Illumination!"

That's what today's celebration is all about: illumination!

It doesn't matter what we do in this life, where we go, what we accomplish, what sufferings we have to endure, provided that we do all things in Christ. He is the light that shines in our darkness, illuminating us from within, making all things bearable.

Delivered at the Church of St. John in Grand Marais on the Second Sunday of Lent March 7, 1993

Thirst, Living Water, and Fulfillment

When I was in the seminary, I had the opportunity to spend five months in Israel with ten of my fellow students. Part of our journey included a five-day trek through the Sinai Desert. It was quite an incredible experience. In addition to being one of the most beautiful places I have ever seen, it was also one big, barren, burnt-out hell-hole. After suffering through five days of intemperate climate in which our guide required us to drink a gallon of water a day, I find it unimaginable to consider how awful it must have been for the Israel-ites to wander in that desert for forty years. I can see why, as in to-day's gospel, they were grumbling at God and cursing at Moses for their lack of water.

When they received water from the rock, it was a different story. They knew God was with them, because he satisfied their needs. He is always appealing to our self-interest, and it is in our self-interest to have our thirsts quenched. You know, in this country we take our water and our thirst pretty much for granted. Turn on the tap and we have an unlimited flow. Reach into a refreshing looking boundary-waters lake, add a halezone tablet and, presto, instant water. It's a far cry from the experience of people in underdeveloped countries who often have to walk three or four miles carrying heavy containers.

I remember back-packing once in the arid mountains of New Mexico. There was so little water there that we had to carry it with us in five-gallon jugs. By the end of the day, as those containers got heavier and heavier, and as I got exhausted from carrying that mis-erable weight around, I would actually curse and swear at the water's mere existence. I surely appreciated its soothing, thirst-quenching properties, though.

Perhaps the greatest drink of water that tourists can enjoy is a cool, refreshing drink from the spring at Wall Drug in South Dakota after spending a few life-draining hours in the hot, arid desert of Bad-lands National Park. In today's gospel, Jesus meets an exhausted, thirsty woman at the town well in Shechem. It is soon apparent that she is not just physically exhausted and thirsty. Her spiritual life has dried up as well. She is looking for the fulfillment of her spiritual needs, and Jesus happens along at just the right time. He provides her with a well-spring of living water to strengthen her for her spiritual journey and to quench her thirst for fulfillment and meaning.

Jesus looks into her soul and helps her find the well inside. It was planted deeply within her when God created her, and all she has to do is confront herself, accept herself for who she is, and acknowledge the presence of God in her life.

You know, when I was younger, and still to some extent now, I was filled with an unquenchable wanderlust, a great desire to escape to distant lands in search of who knows what. Guess what I always find at the end of my journeys? A pot of gold, perhaps? It depends on how you look at it! No matter where I go, I always find the same thing at the end of my search, and that thing is me! It turns out that I am stuck with myself wherever I go! There is no escape. I can't get rid of myself! That's true of most of us, I bet. We all have our ways of trying to escape from who we are, but they are all futile attempts.

As soon as we learn that we have to live with ourselves twenty-four hours a day, we begin to accept ourselves. Life then becomes a satisfying inward journey. You start to look inside to see what's there that you can draw on in your life. And that's when you discover the well that Jesus talks about in today's gospel—a spring of water welling up to eternal life. The reason you find it inside is because God put it there in the first place when you were baptized. He put the light and love of Christ in your heart; and life is no more than coming to discover his presence which has been there from the beginning. If we can acknowledge the presence of Christ within, he becomes the living water that quenches our thirst. That gives us meaning, value, and fulfillment.

There is no more peaceful feeling in the world than to be at peace with God. St. Augustine wrote, "My heart is restless till it rests in God!"

We hear the gospel today and we often think, wouldn't it have been wonderful to meet Christ at the well the way the Samaritan woman did, in which he took the time just to sit and talk and quench all her human desires? The truth is that Christ wants to meet each of us in exactly the same way and be our friend and confidante. He is spiritually present to us whenever we wish. All we need is to take time out to relax, to sit in his presence and respond to his love, anywhere, at any time. We need this because our hearts are little fountains that carry his loving water with us wherever we go.

Let us take a few moments of silence now to sit with Christ, to draw water from his well, and to allow him to quench our thirst for God's love.

Delivered at the Church of St. John in Grand Marais
on the Third Sunday of Lent
March 14, 1993

Mystery, Uncertainty, and Doubt

The man born blind in today's gospel reminds me of another blind man who was this year's retreat master at our annual priests' retreat. He, too, was blind from birth. He told us about a time when he was at a basketball game; he got up to get a Coke at the concession stand and accidentally stumbled out onto the court during an important play. He ran into some of the players and knocked them down. Nobody thought anything of it. They just assumed he was one of the referees.

What was amazing to me about the guy was his attitude. He did not consider his blindness a liability; rather, he considered it an asset. He said it helped him to see important things in life more clearly. He said it taught him to rely on God and that his faith is stronger because of it. It helped him to come to appreciate and love God more deeply. He said it was nice to be a living example to others that life's misfortunes need not be tragic, but instead opportunities to grow spiritually. I concur.

He said that such things are a kind of mud that Jesus rubs into our spiritual eyes to help cure us of our blindness. He said that the word "mud" was actually three capital letters that stood for mystery, uncertainty, and doubt. When we struggle with doubt at uncomfortable times in life, but at the same time allow it, our faith can be strengthened. We come to see what we could not see before.

I love movies where people undergo positive changes in personality, movies in which their experiences help them come to see the light. I love movies in which characters go through critical moments and come out refreshed, renewed, and transformed. They become blessed rather than cursed.

All five nominees for best picture this year are of that nature. But the best of the lot is *Scent of a Woman* in which Al Pacino plays a blind veteran who, at the beginning of the film, is of no use to anyone. He is lonely, bitter, selfish, and rude. He treats everyone with contempt. He even harasses and abuses his pre-school niece and nephew. There is no meaning or value to his existence, and he is not about to let anyone into his life. It's obvious that he is experiencing more than one kind of blindness.

In addition to being physically blind, he is spiritually blind as well, living endless days of despair. An unlikely and unexpected savior comes to him in the form of a high-school senior who baby-sits him for the weekend. The kid helps to open his eyes spiritually. Through the boy's faithfulness, sticking by him in a critical situation when he really needed someone, he learns to find new purpose through other people.

By the end of the movie, you get to like this despicable character a lot. You realize that he may still be physically blind, but he is cured of his spiritual blindness. You leave the theater with a sense of elation and hope for the future. You know that now this guy is going to make the world a better place for a lot of people.

The gospel is full of similar examples in which Christ comes into people's lives, cures their spiritual blindness, helps them see the light, and turns them into instruments of his love to help do his work in the world.

Mary Magdalen was a former prostitute who wept on Jesus' feet and became his most loyal disciple. A man possessed with evil spirits, after being cured, followed Jesus with great enthusiasm. Paul was struck blind on the road to Damascus while persecuting and killing Christians. When he had a vision of Jesus and could see again, he became one of our greatest saints, helping Christ spread Christianity throughout all the Mediterranean world.

The list is endless. In today's gospel we have another example of a blind man whom Jesus called out of darkness into the light by curing him. And how does the beggar respond? He is transformed into a loyal disciple, and he goes off singing God's praises. He even has the courage to take on the whole Jewish court by defending Jesus even though he knows that the Jewish leaders are going to kick him out the door of the synagogue for good.

Sacraments are occasions of healing like that for us. They are special moments to help us see by removing our blindness and transforming us into servants of God.

In baptism we are freed from original sin and born again into God's loving family.

In the Eucharist we come to church as selfish individuals, but leave the church as the Body of Christ, ready to share his love with the world.

In reconciliation we come to God as sinful people in need of spiritual healing. He cures us through the forgiveness of the things that keep us from being better people. When we are forgiven, a weight is lifted, our eyes are opened, we can live life in a new spirit.

In confirmation we receive God's strength through the seven gifts of the Holy Spirit, which allow us to see things more clearly, to follow God more nearly, to love him more dearly.

Today, we have a special group of people with us, young people in high school who are preparing to receive the sacrament of confirmation in May. It's a time in life when a person can really benefit from the loving touch of Jesus Christ. In a few moments, we will celebrate the Second Scrutiny with them.

Today's first reading seems to fit the occasion perfectly. We get still another story of God choosing someone to be his servant in the world. This time it is a teenager he is choosing. We hear the story of the prophet Samuel selecting David to be the king of God's people, the Israelites. The story ends with a description of the sacrament of confirmation.

For us, the great sign of the sacrament is the anointing with oil by the bishop. It is the sign of being chosen and strengthened by God. When Samuel anointed David, it was a sign to all the people that God chose him to be king. A servant of God in the bible is often referred to as "God's anointed one." In fact, the word *Christ* comes from the same word as *chrism*. It means the anointed one.

As the psalm today says, "You anoint my head with oil; my cup overflows. I fear no evil for you are at my side with your rod and your staff that give me courage."

The second sign in confirmation is the laying on of hands. It is the sign that the Holy Spirit is being passed on from one generation to the next. It symbolizes that the Lord is entering our hearts and minds in a very special way. That the Holy Spirit is taking up his home within our bodies. He is present as a source of strength in our calling to the Christian life. As we hear in the story, "from that day on, the Spirit of the Lord rushed on David."

Today's story of David is a touching one. It is a sort of Cinderella story. I'm always for the underdog. David has seven big, burly brothers—great warrior types. Obviously they are excellent material to be kings, the kind of guys you would feel secure with as your leader. But God rejected them all. Samuel asks Jesse, "Have you another son?"

Jesse replies, "No, there's just David, but he's only a kid. He's out tending the sheep."

Ironically, David is the one who is chosen. God works in strange ways sometimes. The reason we can be blind to God is that he sees in ways that we do not see.

This is similar to a story that is about to take place in our parish. Most of us adults have been around the Catholic Church for quite a while. We've faced a lot of spiritual battles in our lives, and have become pretty strong in our faith. Do you think God is choosing us this weekend to do his work? Well, yes. But who does he really need right now?

In today's readings, God is saying, "I want you young people. You are my chosen ones. You are the ones who will help build up my kingdom. Come, follow me!" That is what the sacrament of confirmation is all about, and this weekend he is offering a special invitation to all tenth, eleventh, and twelfth graders of our parish to get ready to receive this sacrament.

On the evening of Saturday, May 8, these young people will be confirmed. It is an exciting time for our parish. It is an event to inspire all of us. When we see young people stand up before us and commit themselves to our faith, it makes our faith come alive right here before our eyes, and helps all of us see God more clearly. I hope everyone of you in our parish sets the evening aside to share in this great sacrament with our young people. They are entering fully into our community of faith. We need each and every parishioner there on that evening to help welcome them into our community of love.

In the gospel today, when the blind man was cured, he went forth and proclaimed his faith in Jesus. Through confirmation, each one of us, too, is to proclaim the faith we have received. Each one of us is called on by God to stand on our own two feet in terms of faith.

When the parents of the blind man were questioned about their son's faith, they replied, "Ask him. He is old enough to speak for himself."

The same can be said about our senior high students, who are old enough to speak for themselves in matters of faith.

Up to now, your faith has been guided and directed by your parents. You were forced into baptism as an infant. Most of you probably cried about it when water was poured on your head. You had very little choice in how you were brought up. Confirmation is a chance for you to say, "Yes, Jesus Christ does have meaning for me in my life. I will accept him. I will follow him. I will serve him as I continue to grow in my faith.''

This is not an easy task. After God chose David, David had to go out and fight a giant named Goliath. You, too, will probably have to face a lot of giants in your spiritual lives. Like the cured blind man who was taunted, jeered, rejected, and looked down upon, you too may be persecuted for your faith at times in your lives. These will be the times in which you will have to cling to Jesus Christ and allow the gift of the Holy Spirit to pull you through.

But between now and May, I want you all to look on this period of time as a happy time in your spiritual lives. Reflect on what an honor it is that God is choosing you in spite of all the weaknesses you have. It's nice to know that God really loves you. That's hard to believe sometimes. The teen years can be pretty turbulent years. Each of you is growing up pretty fast. You're not always sure what is expected of you. You make mistakes. And it's pretty easy to feel badly about things. But have faith. God really loves you through all of this. Look on your Catholic faith as a happy thing, a faith that can bring you real joy. This year you are his chosen people. Even with all your frailties and faults, you are God's special children. Take some time in the next few weeks to really enjoy the fact that, as God sees things, you are the best men and maids of honor in his kingdom.

Delivered at the Church of St. John in Grand Marais
on the Fourth Sunday of Lent
March 21, 1993

Human Tragedy into Divine Glory

The entrance of Jesus into God's holy city is a bitter-sweet moment in his short life. The overwhelming enthusiasm of the crowds makes it a triumphant procession into Jerusalem, but it is just a fleeting moment of glory.

As Samuel said to David's father a couple weeks ago, "Not as man sees, does God see!" God has a kind of glory in mind for Jesus that is much more permanent than a brief procession. In fact the glory that he is planning is eternal.

Jesus told his apostles over and over again that he first had to be lifted high on a cross and undergo suffering and death before he could be truly glorified. And so, today, we begin the great church festival of Holy Week, a mixture of grand elation and extreme sorrow. But, for now, let us celebrate life from a human viewpoint. Let us get caught up in the excitement of this moment as we wave our palm branches enthusiastically and enter the church in a triumphant spirit, praising our messiah and king, the son of David, Jesus Christ, *our Lord.*

For the people of Jerusalem, a week that began in a spirit of triumphant joy has ended in death and confusion and guilt and sorrow. But God sees it all in a different light. He is about to turn human tragedy into divine glory. Let us take a few moments of silence to reflect on what a wonderful God we have who willingly suffered and died for our salvation. And let us pray for the faith to look beyond death with hope in the resurrection to come.

Delivered at the Church of St. John in Grand Marais on Passion (Palm) Sunday April 4, 1993

He Visits Our Tombs with Love
and Calls Us by Name

Today is Palm Sunday. Earlier, at mass, we proclaimed the passion and celebrated the passion and death of Christ on the cross. We are yet awaiting the celebration of his resurrection. If we were the first apostles, we would be totally devastated right now. Our best friend and teacher is dead. We would feel lost, abandoned, cheated, confused, and guilty at the thought of our cowardice and betrayal. We would feel sad and all alone.

But, we have more to go on than the apostles did. We know that Jesus rose from the dead. We know that the death we proclaimed in the Passion this morning is not final. No death is lasting, because Christ has the power to raise us from it as he did his friend Lazarus in last week's gospel.

We come together as people who have sinned. Sin is a form of death, but it is not final either. We trust in God's mercy and forgiveness. Sin makes us feel much like the apostles on the day of Jesus' death—sad, alone, cut off from his love, lost and confused, guilty of our own types of personal betrayal. We are as dead as Lazarus was, wrapped in shrouds of sin, isolated from others by the walls of a smelly tomb. But, we live in the hope that our loving God can change all that. Just as we believe that Jesus rose from the dead, and that he raised Lazarus from the dead, we also believe that he has the power to free us from the death of sin, and raise us to new life in union with God.

He visits our tombs with love and calls us by name: come out, breathe the fresh, new air of forgiveness. Tear down the walls and start to live again.

I don't know if we should hate sin or not. Sure, we should be ashamed of ourselves for committing bad acts, for disobeying God, for failing to love as we should, for mistreating others, or for straying from our principles. But, on the other hand, I think we should also thank God for our sinfulness, because, without it, we would never come to know Christ as our Savior. Our sinfulness gives Jesus a chance to come to our rescue and show us God's infinite, forgiving love. I am grateful to God for many things in my life, but I think the greatest gift I have experienced from him is the forgiveness he brings through Jesus Christ.

There's another kind of dying besides sin. This kind of dying is very important to our growth as Christians. It's the kind of dying that Paul speaks about in today's reading from Philippians. He says that our attitude must be that of Christ. We must have a humble spirit, the frame of mind to empty ourselves, to put God's will ahead of our own desires. In the sacrament of reconciliation, we do just that; we humble ourselves before God, we admit our sinfulness. We let go of our old way of life. We put on Christ and die to our sins.

Such a process is not easy or pleasant. But, the rewards are fantastic. We do it because we believe that Jesus Christ has the power to raise us from the dead, to transform our lives into something new and more wonderful.

As the reading says, "Jesus Christ is Lord!" But, in our dying to self through humility, we once again become his brothers and sisters. We will go on to share in his glory.

Also delivered at the Church of St. John in Grand Marais on Passion (Palm) Sunday April 4, 1993

Our Salvation Is Unfolding Before Us as We Look on in Amazement

Back in ancient days, when the Hebrews were slaves in Egypt, life wasn't too good for them. Oppression was all around, there was terrible suffering, and the Hebrews longed for the day when they would be free again. They believed that God was around somewhere but he surely wasn't doing much. They recalled their glory days when God was a good friend of Abraham, Isaac, Jacob, and Joseph. But where was God now when they really needed him? Why wouldn't he help them? Why did he remain deaf to their cries? Did he care? Did he even exist?

Into this despair God came to his people to rescue them, and worked the greatest miracles that the people had ever seen. He appeared to Moses in the burning bush. He slew the first born of Egypt. He parted the waters and led the people to freedom through the Red Sea. He turned the Hebrews into a great nation at Mount Sinai, and he planted them in the promised land flowing with milk and honey.

These events of the Exodus were the most important in all of Jewish history because now they knew that God cared for them. He was right in their midst, working wonders for them which were beyond belief. They knew now, without a doubt, that God was their God, and they were his chosen people.

These are the events that the Jews celebrate every year at the feast of Passover when they share the paschal meal. Before they left Egypt, Moses instructed the Hebrews to sacrifice a lamb, sprinkle its blood on the door posts, and have a feast inside their houses. God would see the blood, and pass over their homes peacefully. But, he would destroy the firstborn in the Egyptian homes. Though cruel, this is what caused the pharaoh to give the Hebrews their freedom.

The first Passover meal became sacred to the people. It was their Last Supper in slavery and the beginning of their new life as God's people. Every year Jews celebrate this meal, the feast of Passover. When they eat the meal, they recall all the wonderful events which God has done for them.

Passover is more than just remembering old events that happened a long time ago. When they celebrate, eat, and remember, Jews believe that God becomes present to them right now, and that the great events of the past are still unfolding before them in the present.

One of the Jewish prayers in the seder meal says that "on this feast day, each Jew must think of himself as having been personally brought out of Egypt." So the meal is not just a symbolic gesture. The people of the present are part of the salvation of the past, and it is happening to them right now as well.

Because the apostles understood the feast of the Passover so well, it was only natural for Jesus to take this same important meal and give it new meaning as he made it the most important meal that we can celebrate as Christ's followers. Jesus took the Passover meal, and made it his Last Supper which also became the first Eucharist.

Like the Passover meal, the Eucharist is a great memorial meal. We recall the fantastic events which God has worked for us through our Savior, Jesus Christ. Eucharist is a Greek word which means thanksgiving.

Like the Passover meal, when we recall the saving events of the Holy Week—Christ's sacrifice of death on the cross, and resurrection, he becomes present to us in a perfect way. And our salvation is unfolding before us as we look on in amazement.

Just as the Passover was the sacrifice of the lamb, so the Last Supper of Jesus became the celebration of his own sacrifice. He became the Lamb of God himself.

And, as the Passover was the Last Supper that the Hebrews ate in slavery, the Last Supper of Jesus was the final meal eaten in slavery to sin before he won our freedom from sin on the cross.

When I was a little kid growing up in Rochester, Minnesota, we used to travel to Pelican Lake near Brainerd every summer for vacation. We had to pass through St. Cloud on the way, and that was the highlight of the trip, because that's where my grandmother lived. She would always meet us at the door with a hug and kiss, and then she would invite us in for some warm, fresh-baked, homemade bread with strawberry jam (I can just smell it right now). Nobody made bread better than she did. It was the best bread in the whole world.

Well, a few years before she died, she taught my mother her recipe. And now, my mother makes the same kind of bread for me three or four times a year. I expect to have some on Sunday night in Sioux Falls, as a matter of fact. I can't wait!

The point is that every time I eat some of that bread now, I feel like I am ten years old again, and that my grandmother is sitting at the same table with me. The Eucharist is like that. At the Last Supper, Jesus shared bread and wine. He said, "Do this in memory of me!" At every mass, we share this bread in his memory and he becomes present to us like my grandmother is to me when I eat her bread. There is one big difference though. My grandmother is only present in memory and spirit. In the Eucharist, Christ is actually present physically. The bread becomes his physical body. The wine becomes his blood.

At the Last Supper with his closest friends, the apostles, Jesus summed up his life of total giving by sharing bread and wine and conversation with them in a relaxed atmosphere. It was a meal to celebrate his friendship with the apostles. It was a meal to celebrate his undying sacrificial love. It was a meal to celebrate his victory over death before the fact. It was a meal to celebrate over and over again until he would come again.

What boggles my mind is that Jesus knew exactly what he was celebrating, and what was going to happen to him in a few hours. He knew that he was going out to suffer and die for the men that he was eating with. So the Last Supper was more than just a meal with friends. Jesus used it as a sign of total commitment to all people, a sign of the fact that he would be our suffering servant forever, even to the point of death.

He showed this commitment of loving service to others by washing the feet of his apostles. The challenging thing for us as his followers comes to us from the words he speaks after washing their feet, "If I washed your feet, then you must wash each other's feet! What I just did was to give you an example! As I have done, so you must do!"

We are each called to a life of service for others as well. The Eucharist for us, as it was for Jesus, is a sign that we are willing to commit ourselves to suffer on behalf of others. The Eucharist is a sacrament of self-sacrificing love, both on the part of Christ and on the part of his followers.

You may remember these bowls of water from our celebration a few years back. Usually, as you know, on Holy Thursday we get twelve people up here to do as the gospel instructs. I enjoy that ceremony myself. But I am a little too crippled this year to be able to do it properly. So this year it gives us all an opportunity to take part together in the ceremony.

None of us in our western culture washes his feet before supper anymore, but most of us do wash our hands. As a sign of our willingness to follow Christ's words and serve others, we will all have a chance to wash each others hands. I will invite you to come forward in procession to dip your hands into the water to clean them for the Lord's supper. The person ahead of you in line will dry your hands with the towel and then give you the towel so that you can dry the hands of the next person in line behind you. In this way, each one of us will have the opportunity to serve another human being tonight, and we will also be ready to share Christ's feast together with not only clean hands but clean hearts as well.

Delivered at the Church of St. John in Grand Marais on Holy Thursday April 8, 1993

God Blesses Our Suffering

I've been looking forward to celebrating this feast of Good Friday for a couple of months now. It's an extra-special event for me this year because I suspect that it may be my last opportunity to celebrate Christ's crucifixion and death with you. I may still be around next year at this time, but I doubt that I will be able to function as a celebrant then.

All of us have our own little sufferings that we have to endure, and it's nice to have a feast day like this called Good Friday when God blesses our suffering through the suffering of his own son. Our sufferings are minimal compared to the great agony that Jesus had to endure on our behalf to win salvation for us. But our suffering does give us a small taste of his passion and helps us to appreciate at a deeper level the infinite amount of love that God must have for each one of us, for he willingly took on this crucifixion and death as a way to shower his forgiveness and new life on us, even when we really didn't deserve such love in the first place!

Apart from the degree of agony that Jesus had to endure, it occurs to me that there are at least two other major differences between Jesus' suffering and our suffering.

First, most of us wouldn't freely choose our pain or distress. It comes our way naturally whether we like it or not and so we have no choice but to accept it. But Jesus, on the other hand, did not have to suffer if he didn't want to. He freely chose to become a human being. He freely chose to suffer and die for us because he loves us so much.

And the second big difference is that most of us are surrounded by an atmosphere of love in our pain. We have family and friends who care about us. We have people of faith who pray for us and support us spiritually. Those of us who have life-threatening diseases also have doctors and nurses who wish to heal us, so operations are pretty easy to take.

Can you imagine how psychologically terrifying it would be to have an operation performed by someone you thought was trying to severely injure you? When we go to the dentist, we can withstand the pain because we know that he has our best interest at heart.

But Jesus was treated maliciously. He was surrounded by people who hated him and wanted to kill him. They wished to do him bodily harm. Peter and his other friends deserted him when he needed them the most. Judas, his trusted apostle, betrayed him and handed him over to his enemies. The soldiers scoffed at him and made jokes as they whipped him and crowned him with thorns. The psychological pain was much worse than the physical pain and that made the physical suffering even more unbearable.

Jesus' only comfort must have been to see his mother Mary, a few of her friends, and the beloved disciples following him all the way to the cross.

With Christ, we never have to worry about being alone, abandoned, or unloved. He knows what that is like and he doesn't like it one bit. He doesn't want any of us to have to go through it ourselves.

So he surrounds people of faith with a constant atmosphere of love. All we have to do is tap into it through prayer. He is our strength in time of need and our support for any suffering that we may have to endure.

Let us turn to the crucified Christ in a spirit of gratitude and faith as we reflect silently for a few moments on his passion and death. Let us allow his sufferings to transform our sufferings into opportunities for growth and new life.

Delivered at the Church of St. John in Grand Marais on Good Friday
April 9, 1993

New Life Flowing in, Filling Us with Glorious Light

On Thursday evening, at the Last Supper, Jesus told his apostles that he loved them. On Friday, he proved that he loved them with his death on the cross. On Saturday, the apostles learned how much they loved Jesus when they thought they had lost him forever.

And on the first day of the week, Jesus and the apostles came together for the happiest reunion in history. Jesus, who was dead, had come back to life. And even better yet, Jesus was in a good mood! He forgave his friends for their disloyalty. His first words were "Peace be with you!" Their spirits soared and their hearts rejoiced. The apostles gathered around Jesus like children around a birthday cake with lit candles. There was a new life, not only for Jesus but for his friends as well.

Jesus has been alive ever since, dwelling in our hearts as the Savior of the world. This is not just in memory, however; the spirit is an actual entity, helping us to experience Christ's real presence in our lives. Today we share the Easter joy of the first apostles because we feel his resurrection within us. Take a deep breath and feel Christ's love, forgiveness, and new life flowing into our bodies and filling us with his glorious light. Spring is here. Nature is bursting out all over with new life, and Christ has burst out of his tomb and filled our hearts with God's great gift of life.

Tonight, we celebrate that new life in the sacraments. Sean Doucette was born into the world through human parents. Today he will be born into God's family through baptism. He will be washed clean and receive new life.

Dr. Rolph and Laine Linquist will receive the sacrament of confirmation in which the Holy Spirit will strengthen them for their new life in the Catholic Church.

All of us will die to selfishness and rise with Christ in a spirit of loving service through renewal of our baptismal promises and our sharing in the Holy Eucharist.

In a few moments we will share in Sean's joy as he sees the hope of eternal life shine on him from God.

But first I'd like to play the final four minutes of Mahler's first symphony. This music is especially meaningful to me this year after having visited Mahler's summer cabin on the Ottersee in the Austrian Alps where it was written. Mahler described this music as representing a journey from torment to paradise. We'll skip the torment and get right to the paradise stuff. Just sit back and relax and allow this music to lift your spirits and help you share in the glory of Christ's resurrection.

Delivered at the Church of St. John in Grand Marais at the Easter Vigil
April 10, 1993

I Feel Kind of Like Those Two Guys in Today's Gospel

I've just returned from a six thousand-mile vacation, and I think the prettiest scenery I saw on the trip was the North Shore of Lake Superior. I think leaving here for a few days helps me to appreciate the beauty of my own home more.

On the trip I had a chance to do a lot of praying and thinking about my life and I decided that the last year-and-a-half has been the best time of my life. I feel kind of like those two guys in today's gospel. I have come to see Christ a little more clearly in my life through the experience of my illness. God is still a big mystery to me. I don't mean to imply that I have figured him out completely. But I just feel a greater depth to my life and to my faith.

I have always had a rich faith, but it has been very conditional: "God, if you give me this and this and this, then I will do this, and this, and this!" Things have changed slightly now! I trust God more and demand less from him for my satisfaction. I have learned to rely on him more, and I accept better what comes my way. I have felt more intensely the warmth of his friendship and the strength of his support in difficult times. Feelings of peace, security, and joy come to me in times when my life should be in utter turmoil.

In addition to that, on a more down to earth level, I seem to appreciate little things more such as the kindness and encouragement of others. I am more grateful. Consequently, I see God in my daily life more readily. Little things become great spiritual moments as they did in today's gospel in which two disciples enjoy a standard meal with Jesus and have their eyes opened in an ordinary, bare, stone room. They couldn't wait to get back and tell the other disciples.

Easter season is a time for us to share the stories of our own faith, to tell others about how we see Christ present in our lives. As the American bishops tell us, when faith is expressed, it grows and deepens.

98

I hope all of us have had such eye-opening experiences to a greater or lesser degree. That's probably why most of us are here in church today. We have seen Jesus during special moments in our lives. Thus we have a burning desire to come together to celebrate and share his presence among us.

We are still in the heart of the great season of Easter. Christ once died for our salvation. But, he is risen and dwells in our presence through the gift of the Holy Spirit. In the Eucharist, he breaks bread with us and makes his presence known. We see him more clearly than ever. He fills us with his love and sends us out to be his messengers of love to others and to the whole world. To help them see Christ in their presence through us, we must become the sacrament of Christ's presence in the world.

Delivered at the Church of St. John in Grand Marais on the Third Sunday of Easter April 25, 1993

A Life and a Love
That He Wishes Us to Pass on to Others

It's a wonderful image we have of Jesus Christ in the gospel today—the Good Shepherd watching over us, protecting us, guiding us through life, standing with us in times of need as our strength, security, and support.

I love Psalm 23 which talks about God as being our support during the dark moments of our lives: "Though I walk through the valley of death, I fear no evil, for you are at my side with your rod and staff that give me courage!" I think those words are often misunderstood, though. Some people think that if they have enough faith, they can avoid suffering, that somehow Christ can keep life from hurting. But that is not the message I get from the second reading today.

Peter suggests that our suffering is acceptable to God. Life is full of unpleasant things: fear, worry, sorrow, anger, loneliness, physical and mental anguish. We can't escape it. With faith, we still have those things in our lives. But, we also have a special friend to share them with us, a friend who understands because he has been through them as well. That friend is Jesus Christ, our Savior, who suffered and died on the cross for our salvation. Jesus Christ can't take away the tough or painful things in your life, but he can be there with you and give you courage and make you feel a little more secure.

In the second reading St. Peter discusses the role of suffering in the Christian life. He should know. Peter was a real authority on the subject. He gave up everything he had to follow Jesus. He even went to Rome and was crucified to death, upside down, because he loved Jesus so much. He must have died a happy man. Peter is like this Minnesota Twins doll, smiling in the face of adversity, humiliation, and defeat because he is a loyal fan and can take the rough, little setbacks.

If any of you are experiencing difficult times in life right now, I would suggest that you read the two books of Peter in the New Testament. They are the best books of all. They are both very short, easy to read, and carry a wonderful message. Peter says that you can't escape suffering in life, so why try? In fact, since you have to suffer anyway, why not do it for Jesus Christ and glorify his name through it.

I think that's a beautiful thought. Listen again to Peter's words from today's second reading: "If you put up with suffering for doing what is right, this is acceptable in God's eyes. It was for this that you were called, since Christ suffered for you in just this way and left you an example to have you follow in his footsteps."

Suffering for Christ in a spirit of thankfulness and recompense brings to mind a true story in British history. A few decades after the Norman conquest of England, under the reign of King Henry I, there lived a feudal Lord in the north named Sir Roger Teechkborn. He ruled his lands with an iron fist and cared little about the well-being of the peasants. He was much like the sheriff of Nottingham from the Robin Hood movie in that he was merciless, stubborn, cruel, sadistic, selfish, and vain. He's probably the one who really said "No more table scraps for the poor!"

Sir Roger had a wife named Lady Maybella who was just the opposite of himself. She was charitable and a woman of deep faith. The struggling poor would often come to her for help behind her husband's back to whom she responded with a loving spirit of great generosity. After a long life filled with good deeds toward the poor, Lady Maybella lay on her deathbed. She had no fear of death, but she was troubled by the thought of the distress which would fall on the poor of the village when they could no longer come to her for help.

She pleaded with her husband Sir Roger to set aside a piece of land large enough to produce wheat, which would provide enough bread to feed the poor. In his sadistic way, Sir Roger agreed to grant his dying wife's request on one condition. Grabbing a blazing stick from the open hearth, he held it aloft and harshly declared that he would set aside as much land for the poor as the Lady Maybella could walk around while the flame continued to burn.

Remember, this is a true story. To his amazement, she jumped out of her deathbed, grabbed the torch, and began her march. It turned into a crawl as she could hardly muster enough strength to even move. She had a major dilemma: she knew she could crawl around a small bit of land, but that would not be enough to take care of the great needs of the poor. If she tried a bigger stretch, she might not have the strength to finish and close the circle.

She offered a prayer to God for strength and went for the big one. She painfully dragged herself along the ground and miraculously circled an area of twenty-three acres for the poor. Sir Roger was so moved by her personal sacrifice that he kept his promise to her, even after she was dead and gone. That was almost nine hundred years ago, and to this day that stretch of land is used to produce grain that goes solely to help make bread for the poor.

The local people have a special name for that stretch of land. They call it "The Crawls" in honor of the Lady Maybella and how she died to give bread to the poor. It reminds us of Jesus Christ, falling down three times as he carried his cross up the hill of Calvary. The burning torch is like the Easter candle, reminding us that Christ is the light of the world. As Lady Maybella died to give bread to the poor, so Jesus died on the cross to give his body and blood, the bread of life and the cup of eternal salvation, to the poor in spirit.

Each one of us is spiritually hungry. We need the spiritual bread that Jesus offers each one of us. He gives us strength, courage, peace, joy, and spiritual fulfillment, to name just a few things. Jesus and Lady Maybella should inspire each one of us. Jesus encourages us to take on suffering and sacrifice for the good of others. The Eucharist should make us less selfish, help us to love others more, and care for the needs of those who are hurting. Jesus loves each one of us very much. He proved his love by dying on the cross for us.

But this is Easter. He is no longer dead. He is alive and well and living within our hearts. He asks us to be his body. To do his work in the world. To take on a bit of suffering for those in need. Jesus' last words in today's gospel are these: "I came that you might have life, and have it to the full!" In a few minutes, we will all come forward to receive his body and blood, to feel his love in our hearts, and experience his life to the full, a life and a love that he wishes us to pass on to others.

Delivered at the Church of St. John in Grand Marais on the Fourth Sunday of Easter May 2, 1993

The Greatest Act of Love

It's fairly obvious from the first reading today that right from the very beginning the Church couldn't make it without lots of volunteers. In the Acts of the Apostles we see the leaders of the Church picking volunteers to help wait on tables. Ever since that time the Church has been strong more because of its lay people than because of its clergy. It takes both clergy and laity working together under the unity of the Holy Spirit to make the body of Christ an effective instrument in spreading Christ's love.

Last night, I was in total awe of our parish as the bishop came to help us celebrate confirmation. I felt very proud as I saw all the sponsors and parents who worked so hard over the last couple years to prepare our young people for the sacrament. I was very inspired by the love and devotion Marilyn Duffy put into organizing the program. Many more volunteers worked many more hours decorating the church, mastering the music, and preparing a great banquet. It was a truly wonderful parish celebration. I can say the same thing about last week when we celebrated First Communion. I am grateful to Judy Peterson, Cathi Williams, all the grade-school teachers, volunteers, and parents who made the church sparkle with decorations, music, food, and the great loving spirit of Jesus Christ.

I could rattle on for hours about how grateful I am to almost every person in our community for the wonderful things they do for our parish family. It's been true from the very beginning, but I am especially appreciative now that I am sick. It's nice to see that you all love Christ and his Church as much as you do your own families.

The parish council is putting on an appreciation dinner on May 19 to thank you all. Bob and Martha Pye have invited us to their house and beach for a hot dog roast. Please set the date aside. I hope you can all make it as there is no agenda, no expectations, and no responsibility, just a chance to relax and enjoy each other's company for a few peaceful moments by the sea.

Today, as a nation, we honor another group of volunteers: mothers. We know what it means to live a Christian way of life because we have been taught much by our mothers: selfless loving, dedication to others, self-sacrifice, looking out for the needs of others, and cultivating a generous spirit. I was uplifted the other day when I saw a mother pushing a baby buggy down the street. It was a simple act, but I thought, "This is the most important thing that human beings can do; a mother taking time to be with her children and nurture them is perhaps the greatest act of love."

Church documents speak about how parents are the most important factor in helping children come to faith. And Jesus Christ could never save the world without the love of mothers. In fact, Jesus Christ needed Mary, his mother, to nurture him and help him grow up to be our Savior in the first place.

When I was in my last couple years of high school, I thought there were too many rules around home. I couldn't wait to graduate so I could move out and live my own life, independent and free.

Well, the day came; I became my own man at long last. I moved away to college. Two weeks later, I wanted to come back home. I missed my mother. But I knew I could never go back home again. A few days visit, yes! But childhood was over. I wish I had appreciated my parents more at the time I was growing up with them.

Mothers get kind of a bum deal. When the kids are around, they're not quite old enough or responsible enough to appreciate all that their mothers do for them. Moms are pretty much taken for granted. When kids finally realize the great sacrifices of motherhood, they're gone for good, off raising their own families.

I guess that's what Mother's Day is for—a chance to show our gratitude in a special way for our mother's love in the form of a card, gift, or a phone call.

I guess the message I want to leave with you mothers is that when you feel a bit down and unappreciated, remember that God knows, cares, and appreciates all that you do from the bottom of his heart. You're the most important volunteers that he's got to help his kingdom grow. And today's gospel says that all your efforts will be rewarded. He's gone off to heaven to prepare a special place for you with Mary his mother where you can talk over your joys and sorrows in a peaceful atmosphere. God bless you all, and have a happy Mother's Day.

Delivered at the Church of St. John in Grand Marais on the Fifth Sunday of Easter May 9, 1993

We Can Be Instruments of Christ's Love

When the apostles go to Samaria, in the first reading, they lay their hands upon some new converts and pray that they may receive the Holy Spirit. It reminds us of the wonderful celebration of confirmation that we enjoyed last week with the bishop who laid his hands upon our high school students and helped them to receive the gifts of the Holy Spirit.

We've had some great parish parties the last couple of weeks: first communion two weeks ago, confirmation last week, and next week we will be honoring our graduating seniors. Those kinds of occasions really make a parish come alive, just like in the Acts of the Apostles where it says that "the rejoicing in that town rose to a fever pitch."

Life at St. John's has been pretty intense lately. Once again I'd like to thank Marilyn Duffy, Judy Peterson, Cathi Williams, Linda Delonais, Mary Ann Skadberg, Jean Riley, the teachers, sponsors, parents, musicians, laborers, volunteers, the congregation, the children, the junior and senior high school students, the bishop, and Jesus Christ himself, for all your help. It was a lot of fun for me, and I am grateful to you all. Please join us for an appreciation hot dog roast out at the Pye home on Thursday night after the mass for the Feast of the Ascension.

Last week, we enjoyed hearing the Bishop point to the stained glass window and mention how, when Jesus was baptized in the Jordan River, a voice came from heaven which said, "You are my beloved son; in you I am well pleased!" He mentioned that our baptisms were also a sign of God's pleasure, that we, too, are his sons and daughters, and that his love for us is ever present and everlasting.

Well, I'm happy to say that the bishop is going to speak with us again today. Unfortunately, he is not live but on tape. Today our United Catholic Appeal Drive kicks off. You will all be receiving donation and pledge cards in the mail. Please give generously. This is our yearly opportunity to show our gratitude to the bishop and support our diocese with all of its essential programs which help Christ do his work in the world.

We can be instruments of Christ's love as well, but it takes sacrifice on our part. We can become instruments of Christ's love by enthusiastically assisting our diocese with our prayer and our urgently needed financial support. The assessment for our parish this year is $8,803, a goal which we must meet, and can only meet, if you all demonstrate a spirit of profound sacrifice.

I'd like to speak for a few moments about a special organization and a special person in that organization. You remember the NET Team of young, college-aged Christians who come to our parish every year to put on a retreat for our junior and senior high school students. Each year they have inspired our young people and raised the spirits of our parish. We are grateful to them in ways we can never repay. Today, we have the opportunity to show our gratitude in a small way.

The NET Team does not have a storehouse of funds on which to draw. They can only survive on the generosity and support of individual Christians like us. Each member of the team must do some fund raising to help pay his or her own way. To assist them in this regard, each member has a sponsor parish to give support through prayer and donations. I am pleased today that Sharon Gregory from our parish has been accepted on the team for next year. We know from seeing how helpful she has been around our parish and from witnessing her strong personal faith that she is going to be a great asset to the NET Team and to Christ. She has a generous spirit, especially with her time, and has done a lot to help us have a good youth program this year at St. John's.

Today is our chance to show her a little appreciation and to help support her work next year as she journeys with NET to hundreds of parishes throughout the United States and the rest of the world. After just hearing about UCA, you may be a bit distressed that we are taking up another collection today. But just remember how your generous spirit enriches the lives of others. Today you have the chance to double your happiness. Sharon would like to speak to us for a few moments and then we will take up a collection on her behalf.

Delivered at the Church of St. John in Grand Marias on the Sixth Sunday of Easter May 16, 1993

I Call You to Christ, to Live in His Love, Today and Forever

When I was a kid growing up in Rochester, at the age of about nine or ten, there was an old, abandoned house across the street that was to be torn down to make a parking lot. One summer day, before it was demolished, my brothers and I went over to explore the thing. We sneaked inside and discovered that it was gutted. The walls were bare. All the furniture was gone. We went upstairs and found a room that still had a few carpets on the floor. That room became our secret clubhouse for the next few days before they tore the house down.

We told a few trusted friends about it, and we all went up there and just sat around for hours and told stories every day for about five days. Then workers came and tore the house down, and our clubhouse was gone forever. But, for a time, it was the center of our lives, and we became very close friends because of it. That room and those peaceful days spent in it have been an important part of my memories ever since.

Today's reading from the Acts of the Apostles reminded me of that old room. The apostles spent nine days in such an upper room themselves. A secret hideaway where they could be safe and alone. For them it was a nine-day novena spent with Jesus' mother, Mary, and a few other women. It was a time of prayer, of recalling Christ's activity in their lives, of telling stories of his great deeds, of remembering his most important words to them, a time to pray for the gift of the Holy Spirit who was about to come into their lives in a dramatic way.

If their experience was anything like my childhood clubhouse days, the nine days they spent in that upper room must have brought them very close together and cemented their friendship for life. No wonder they were so open and receptive to the Holy Spirit when he finally came. Eventually they would leave the upper room for good, but in deeper union with each other and with Jesus, unified in a spirit of confidence and determination to continue Christ's work in the world.

But, for now it was just a time to relax, stay out of view of the authorities, and enjoy each other's company in private. In many ways, our gathering is like that today. We are sharing time together in a space where we can just sit and worship as we please without fear of government restrictions. We come together in faith to share friendship as brothers and sisters in Christ, to support each other in our prayer, to remember the stories of Jesus, and to share them out loud together over and over again. We do this Sunday after Sunday, year after year. We do this to reflect on his words and allow them to transform our lives; we also receive him in the Eucharist and allow his Holy Spirit to strengthen us so that we might better, as Peter puts it in the second reading, embrace suffering with a spirit of joy, as that we may leave this place to share Christ's love with the world. But there is a danger in all this—that our friendship and faith might become selfish, inward-directed, stagnant, and inactive. To avoid that, we must always be thinking outwardly.

Once upon a time, a group of people in a coastal Maine town with a treacherous shoreline built a lighthouse to save people from crashing their boats on the dangerous rocks. Everyone who joined the group knew that their commitment was to sacrifice their own comfort on dark, stormy nights to rescue people in peril.

They were all dedicated at first. But, after a while, they decided that the monthly meetings were more fun. They decided that not all of them should have to go out to the lighthouse on cold nights. So they sent a few people out on their behalf to operate the lighthouse.

A few months later, at one of their meetings, they decided that all of them could stay home as they hired one man to do their work. Thus they could just keep the light bright so people in danger could find their way. A few months later they decided that the meeting room in the lighthouse needed more carpeting. So to conserve funds they fired the lighthouse keeper and turned down the intensity of the light. Eventually, they turned out the light completely. They only turned it on as a signal to call members together for their meetings.

A year later, in the middle of the night, some disgruntled villager quietly changed the sign above the door from ''lighthouse'' to ''clubhouse''!

What a group. I guess the moral of the story is that if we exist as a community just for ourselves, we are not the Church of Christ.

We are all just wasting our baptisms. The Catholic Church is much more than just a club that we belong to. It is a sign of Christ's saving love in the world. We are called to be his light to the nations. Our baptisms are an affirmation that we are part of a group that has committed itself to the suffering work that helps bring Christ's love to every person on earth.

The apostles, under the guidance and the strength of the Holy Spirit, eventually left the security of the upper room for good, and went out to proclaim the good news to the world and establish Christ's Church. Through our baptism and confirmation, we are called by Christ to continue their work.

I'd like to say a few words in closing to the graduates today. This is a special group to me because they were the first class of fifth graders that I ever had here for release time. At the time, I thought they were a bunch of little, squirrelly kids in class. It's been fun to see them grow up and become big, squirrelly kids.

I've had a lot of fun with Pat, Mitch, and Jenny over the years and I'm going to miss you all a lot. Jason came on the scene a little later, so I haven't gotten to know you quite as well. But, I really enjoyed your presence in our confirmation class because you brought some freshness and honesty to it.

I especially want to thank the four of you for your enthusiasm and for being such good examples to the younger kids in the parish. I was amazed last year at your dedication and loyalty to the program. I want to thank Pat and Mitch for being real leaders to the young people in our parish. I really appreciated your being group moderators for our sexuality program. I think the younger kids really appreciated it, too.

The four of you are kind of in the same situation of the apostles in today's readings. They had the security of Jesus being with them for three years. Now he was gone and ascended into heaven. They were suddenly on their own. They had to look toward the future with a sense of fear and uncertainty but, also, with an adventurous spirit.

You, too, are in a time of transition. You've had the security of family and friends of a small, personal-sized school with teachers who really care. Now you're going off on your own. You have to exchange the security blanket of home for an uncertain new world. It's scary, but it's also exciting. It can be a new adventure to give depth and meaning to your lives. Like the apostles, if you carry the spirit of Christ that you received from the bishop at confirmation with you, then you can be at home wherever you go. Along with Christ, you can carry the spirit of your parents with you too. You'll be amazed at how you can never get them out of your system. You'll carry them and Christ with you forever.

This summer a number of young people from our parish will be going out to Denver to see the Pope. He meets the youth of the world once a year on World Youth Day, and we are starting to get excited about being part of it. The Pope always has some wonderful things to say, and in closing I'd like to read a few of his words from one former such gathering:

> Everywhere, young people are asking important questions, questions on the meaning of life, on the right way to live, on the true scale of values. These questions bear witness to your thoughts, your conscience, your hearts and wills. This questioning tells the world that you young people carry within yourselves a special openness with regard to what is good, and what is true. To each one of you, I say, therefore, heed the call of Christ when you hear him saying to you: "Follow me! Walk in my path! Stand by my side! Remain in my love!" There is a choice to be made. A choice for Christ and his way of life, and his commandments of love. So to all of you, I extend, in the name of Christ, the call, the invitation, the plea: "Come and follow me!" I call you to Christ, to live in his love, today and forever. Amen.

Delivered at the Church of St. John in Grand Marais on the Seventh Sunday of Easter May 23, 1993

Seeds of the Kingdom

Praised be God,
the Father of our Lord Jesus Christ,
the Father of mercies,
and the God of all consolation!
He comforts us in all our afflictions
and thus enables us
to comfort those who are in trouble
with the same consolation
we have received from him.
As we have shared much
in the suffering of Christ,
so through Christ
do we share abundantly in his consolation.

2 Corinthians 1:3-5

Peril, Paleontology, and the True Meaning of Life

Dear Commodore Greenwell and Green River Grifters
(aka Griping Rafters):

My prayers are with you all as you risk your lives on the rapids, or by placing your safety in the hands of Bob Greenwell. I hope you will have a great time. I wish I were part of it all. But I won't be depressed about missing it. I've been on three such trips already with my brother, John, and each one has provided me with unforgettable memories. I'm just happy that all of you will experience what I have enjoyed immensely in the past: spectacular scenery, exciting rapids, good company, thirst-quenching beer, relaxing and peaceful wilderness, godawful heat, and the pleasure of carting all kinds of stuff around wherever you go!

I'm sitting comfortably in front of the TV set watching *The Ten Who Dared* and having a glass of wine in your honor. Here's mud in your eye, or all over your body, from the sandy depths of the Green River after it has just flowed out of *Jurassic Park* to the northeast.

The following is a portion of my Father's Day homily. I thought some of you might get a kick out of it.

Jeremiah is constantly complaining to God about his terrible treatment by the people he serves. But he endures the discomfort because he is totally dedicated and loyal to his God. His confidence in God is utterly astounding. Though his world is falling apart around him and he is besieged on every side, he still knows that God is always with him and fighting his battles for him. He knows that he has no need to tremble or fear.

Jeremiah's ranting kind of reminds me of my own father back in the days when he was raising nine kids. As we would all be at each others' throats, he would turn his head toward heaven and pray: "Oh, Lord, give me strength to bear up under the strain of all these children!" I suppose most of you dads can identify with my dad's prayer.

Being a father is a full-time responsibility. It takes fidelity in difficulty, and commitment in times of suffering.

I had the opportunity to witness that kind of dedication last week when I visited my sister Mary and her husband Bob in San Francisco. We all sat down to relax and watch a movie on TV. However, Bob could not relax because he had to get up seven or eight times to look after his four-year-old son Danny. Earlier in the day, we were on the seventeen-mile drive in Monterey. We stopped at the cypress tree lookout. Danny wanted to get out of the car to look at the contorted tree. His father said he had better just look at it from the car. Without knowing what I was doing, I persuaded Bob to let his son get out of the car. That was my big mistake. After we got back to the car, they tried to buckle him into his safety restraints, and this precipitated an awful tantrum that lasted more than ten minutes. What did I learn from this experience? First, I learned not to stick my nose where it doesn't belong; and second, I learned that there are many advantages to being a celibate priest!

As men of faith, you know that, like Jeremiah the prophet, God is with you to help you in your Christian vocations as dads. My dad's prayer for strength always seemed to do him a lot of good. It helped him to retain his composure so that he could be more patient, caring, and understanding. His prayer helped us kids, too. No matter what his faults were, we knew he was a man of faith, dedicated to his family and to his wife. It gave us all a feeling of great security even when we didn't always see eye to eye on things. Even though our dad spent most of his life at work, when he came home, he always made us feel like we were more important to him than his job.

There is an old joke about the father who let his son take out the car alone for the first time in his life. When the kid came back several hours later, his father asked him how it went. The kid said, "Well, I've got some good news and some bad news." The father said, "You better give me the good news!" The kid responded, "Well, um, er, the um, the air bags really work great."

Needless to say, the father was furious inside, but he managed to retain some degree of composure on the outside. He was thinking to himself, "Kids! Life would be so much easier without them."

Easier, yes, but more meaningful? I doubt it. Parenthood is the greatest responsibility in life. It is probably also God's greatest gift. Commitment to children really fills our lives with purpose, meaning, and a sense of being needed.

This commitment seems to be one of the major themes in Steven Spielberg's *Jurassic Park*! At the beginning of the film, the paleontologist, Sam Neill, doesn't want to get married and have children. He says they are noisy, unclean, and can't sit still like his fossils do; and, when children are little, they stink. But when he sees live dinosaurs running around in the park, his life of digging up fossilized bones from the past ceases to have any meaning. He discovers that the true meaning of his life comes from a commitment to living beings in the present—especially to children.

When another adult, who is in charge of two kids at the park, flees in terror from a rampaging tyrannosaurus, leaving them in peril, the paleontologist suddenly finds that he is stuck with the kids whether he likes it or not. The children don't trust *him* either, saying, "That other guy deserted us! Is that what you'll do, too?" Sam Neill is forced to say, "I will stay with you no matter what happens!" It makes the kids feel secure when they really need it. Anyway, through his total commitment to the kids, the paleontologist discovers that they aren't so bad after all, and the implication is that he wants some kids of his own.

Jesus tells us in today's gospel to be his witnesses in the world. When he asks us not to be silent, I don't think he necessarily means that we have to stand out on street corners to rant and rave like a lunatic at the University of Minnesota. Christ is more interested in action than words. To become his followers he means for us to offer ourselves in personal sacrifice—to be people of committed love for each other.

Today we honor our fathers. You are men who live out Christ's message by being committed to your children even when it is difficult. Your love, like God's, is forgiving, eternal, and unconditional. It is based on self-sacrifice rather than on personal satisfaction or reward. And, like Jeremiah, if you accept your fatherly vocation in a spirit of faith, you will have the confidence, support, and strength which comes from your own father in heaven who will never desert you in time of need.

Well, that's about it. I had two goals this year: one was to visit every brother and sister at home, and the second was to go rafting in July. I completed the first goal and enjoyed every minute of it. I will fulfill the second vicariously through you. Have a great time.

I will see you all at Gull Lake for Dad's birthday celebration. God bless you and grant you happy trails!

Love,

Max Horse!

A letter to participants in a river-rafting trip
July 1993

More Important Than a Whole Flock of Sparrows

When the walls came down in Eastern Europe a couple of years back, it was wonderful to see the Orthodox priests celebrating their faith right outside in the open squares after having been suppressed for so many years by the state. It is ironic that, in America, where we have freedom of speech and freedom of religion, most of us are afraid to admit in public that Jesus Christ is an important part of our lives.

Faith seems so private and personal to us. If it came down to martyrdom, I'll bet many of us would have courage enough to die out of love and loyalty to Christ. But we would rather not mention his name if it might cause us some embarrassment or discomfort in our normal, daily lives. In today's gospel Jesus instructs us not to remain silent. The world needs his love and his good news to help redeem it. And if that good news is not delivered by his best friends, where is it going to come from?

Originally, the word *martyr* had nothing to do with death or suffering. In Greek it simply means *witness*. We are called by Christ to be his witnesses in the world. That is not an easy task. It usually means some form of suffering on our parts to get the message across. To stand up for Christ in the modern world often carries with it the threat of ridicule and unpopularity—perhaps, on occasion, persecution and, in extreme cases, even death. But in all of this we have those reassuring words in the middle of the gospel. God knows, cares, and is with us through it all. Each one of us is more important to him than a whole flock of sparrows—and God knows each sparrow personally.

Part of the Homily Delivered at the Church of St. John in Grand Marais
on the Twelfth Sunday of the Church Year
June 20, 1993

Experts of Hospitality at Work

I just got back from a twenty-five day vacation which gave me the opportunity to support one of our nation's biggest industries, the motel business. These people are experts at hospitality, welcoming you with a friendly smile, helping you to relax and be comfortable after a grueling day on the road. Of course, they have the ulterior motive of making a profit. But, as Jesus says in today's gospel, "He who welcomes a prophet, receives a prophet's reward!"

I also had the opportunity to see other experts of hospitality at work: the National Park Rangers. They, too, were friendly and helpful. I can't say I was surprised though, having come to know the Forest Rangers in our own parish. Wherever I went, they all reminded me of the friendly community of public servants we have back here at home. Many of you work as ushers at St. John's as well. I am grateful to you for all the work you do at weekend Masses to help our visitors feel welcome and appreciated.

There's something special about the Grand Marais community in general. Maybe it's the small-town atmosphere. I've always felt good about it. It didn't take me long, as a complete stranger, to feel welcomed here, and in a very short time to think of this place as my life-long home.

Unfortunately, in our modern world, it's dangerous to trust complete strangers. A number of families in our parish have been totally devastated by violence by people unknown to them. Such incidents create a justifiable and healthy fear of transient people. Providing home and personal protection and security has become a multi-billion dollar business in the United States.

I remember, last year, when I got into some trouble on the highway. I saw a light shining in the woods, coming from a house, so I hiked in to ask for some help. I knocked on the door, which was bolted. There was no answer. I saw a terrified woman sitting at the kitchen table. I showed her my Roman collar through the window. I didn't blame her for not trusting even a priest. I asked her if she would dial 911 for me. She did. I waited in my car for the highway patrol to come out and rescue me. I thought this lady was a very wise woman, even though she really had nothing to fear from me.

It is inspiring to read about the old couple in the first reading with the generous spirit, welcoming Elijah into their home and providing for all his needs. It reminds us of all those times in our lives when people have come to our assistance. These experiences create a feeling of gratitude in us toward God and the people he sends to help us in time of need.

Delivered at the Church of St. John in Grand Marais
on the Thirteenth Sunday of the Church Year
June 27, 1993

Glorious Opportunities for God to Speak

When Isaiah wrote about the rain, he obviously never spent any time in the Midwest. To him, rain was life-saving. Out in the wastelands of Israel, a good rain shower could transform a parched, arid desert into plush, green, rich, fertile land. Irrigation in the Jordan Valley brings forth delicious fruits and vegetables even today.

In the beautiful oasis, people pray for the banks of the Jordan River to overflow. Isaiah says that God's word behaves in the same way: watering our barren lives, enriching our existence, helping us to bring forth spiritual fruits. It's a different story this year in the Mississippi River Valley. Too much rain has caused much flooding. Our hearts and prayers go out to the millions of people whose lives have been devastated by the floods. It's a terrible thing—high raging waters washing away the top soil and any people who get in the way, turning peoples' homes and possessions into mud, drowning the farm fields and suffocating the seeds, which causes farmers to go bankrupt. Instead of bringing forth life, incessant rain can snuff it out. Too much rain is just as bad as too little.

The question cropped up in my mind: could the same be true of the word of God? Can we get too much of it? Is saturation a dangerous thing? You bet it is! Jesus, in his gospel parable, failed to mention a fourth adverse growing condition, that too much water saturates, suffocates, and destroys seeds. I personally think that it is possible for some people to get too much of the word of God, too much Bible. They get saturated with it, often adding an unhealthy, fundamentalist approach to their understanding of scripture. The mind ceases to be a fertile ground for rational thought. The mind narrows extremely in focus, closing out any insight which God may wish to plant there. A healthy mind seeks a proper balance among many sources of information so that we can contrast and compare ideas, expanding our horizons with other people's thought.

The truth is that God's Word comes to us in many ways, and the Bible is just one of those sources. God didn't stop communicating with us the day that the last word of the Bible was written down.

He continues to speak to us, not only through tradition and Church authority, but through our faith and emotions, through reflection on life experiences, and through the rational thought processes that help us to assimilate knowledge from the many sources available to us from the world around us. If we saturate our thinking with only Bible study, we choke off all those other glorious opportunities for God to speak to us in our hearts.

In addition to the danger of developing a narrow-minded focus which can evolve from relying on only one source of information, another danger comes to mind: fanaticism. These two dangers go hand in hand. People tend to start thinking in one way. They develop a rigid system of thought. When ideas come along that threaten their logic structures, they react violently against the intrusion. You see this in people who refuse to be open to the theory of evolution. They won't even consider logical, scientific evidence. They try to distort empirical data with wild claims. They fight to keep rational thought out of their children's schools.

The Church has been guilty of this narrow, fanatical focus from time to time. Using a telescope that he built himself, Galileo discovered a number of moons orbiting around Jupiter. The mere existence of those moons refuted an age-old historical argument extending back to the time of Aristotle. It was enough evidence to prove to Galileo that Copernicus was correct: all the planets, including the earth, revolve around the sun. The Church, however, was not impressed. The biblical world view, that the sun and planets revolved around the earth, was challenged.

It took the Church three hundred and fifty years to make a posthumous apology to Galileo. Scientists can be guilty of this too. Sometimes, emotional biases cause them to spike their own empirical data or conclude that a colleague may be off his rocker. The scientific world refused to accept Freud's theories for years. They thought that Einstein's theories of relativity were too far-out to be true until his ideas started clearing up and explaining some important physical anomalies, like the orbital glitch of the planet Mercury.

When I was in high school, scientists were scoffing at the ideas of continental drift and plate tectonics. Now these ideas are the very foundation of modern geological thought. Today, anybody in his or her right mind has to conclude that the theory of evolution is a scientific fact. But you won't find that conclusion in people who base their thinking purely on the first two chapters of Genesis. Fortunately, in 1943, Pope Pius XII published a papal encyclical entitled *Divino Afflante Spiritu* to help foster the growth of biblical studies. His basic premise was that the mind is a terrible thing to waste. God has given us the power of rational thought and we should use it to get a better handle on Scripture. He mentions that we need to use other disciplines such as archeology, paleontology, history, sociology, psychology, and physics, among others, to help us grow in our appreciation and understanding of the Bible.

Shutting out those other forms of education leads to fanaticism which doesn't do anybody any good. It creates an environment where there is no chance for communication. People tend to talk right past each other without listening. They become irrational and frustrated, often turning to unloving behavior in an attempt to foist their beliefs on others. They often become hateful and bitter towards others, which can result in extreme anger, violence, destruction to property, manslaughter, or even pre-meditated murder.

What am I saying here today? Am I refuting the Bible? Am I ignoring today's readings? I don't think so! I am just pleading for balance in education so we aren't taken in by another James Jones or David Koresh, or Ervil Labaron, or Charles Manson, each of whom used the Scriptures expertly in a selfish way to get the power they wanted over people. I personally love the Bible, as does the Catholic Church. It is sacred to us. In any published Church document, there are always many quotes cited from the Bible as a basis for important thoughts. But, our official Church teaching does not arise out of a vacuum. It begins in an atmosphere of prayer, but is developed through reflection on the real world in which we exist.

I love the Bible. It is a great book. I love reading it and reflecting on it. The weekly readings are always my starting point for reflecting on what I want to say in my homilies. To me, the Scriptures are the foundation of all God's truth. I think the Bible is loaded with unbelievably inspiring thoughts. Take the second reading from Paul today. I am a man with a terminal disease, and I can't think of any more beautiful thought for people in my situation than the words inspired by God and written down by St. Paul. They give me the hope to look beyond my present situation to a better life ahead. They encourage me to trust that God is slowly working out his plan for each one of us. Listen to his words again:

Consider the sufferings of the present to be nothing compared with the glory to be revealed in us. Indeed, the whole created world eagerly awaits the revelation of the children of God. We ourselves, although we have the spirit as first fruits, groan inwardly while we await the redemption of our bodies.

How could anybody not fall in love with beautiful words like that? I indeed love the Bible. I would recommend it to everyone. Read from it for a few minutes every day and then reflect on what you read. But please, look for God's word to you from other sources as well.

Delivered at the Church of St. John in Grand Marais
on the Fifteenth Sunday of the Church Year
July 11, 1993

Little Seeds of the True Kingdom of God

Well, that's one side of the kingdom—the people of God forming a community based on self-sacrificing love. The other side has to do with God and how he treats us. He's like the benevolent government. He listens, he cares, and he responds to us in our need. He has many great qualities. He is all-powerful, all-knowing, and all-loving. In the gospel today, Jesus offers three parables describing the kingdom of God. I'd like to offer four more of my own to the list.

The kingdom of God is the entire population of a small town on the Mississippi River working together to save their neighbors from total devastation. The kingdom of God is people from all over the country with generous spirits, sending money thousands of miles to people they do not even know; this demonstrates that they are with them in spirit in their time of suffering. The kingdom of God is a government responding with a caring ear and financial support to help the victims of disaster in their need.

Other recent examples that come to mind are the San Francisco earthquake a few years back, the hurricane in Florida last year, and the flooding of the Mississippi River Valley this year. I don't think we should take this benevolent government for granted, especially when you look at the leadership of such countries as Somalia and Yugoslavia, which seem to exist only to cause outrageous suffering in the lives of their people. Finally, the kingdom of God is where the National Guard brings love, protection, and peace, rather than bullets, fear, and war.

What's amazing to me is how people whose lives are devastated can bring out the best qualities in human nature. One lady on the news spoke about how important her faith in God was to help bring a feeling of security to her uncertain future. Our faith in a benevolent God is what makes the kingdom possible for us on this earth. He is watching over us with a constant, protective spirit.

In the first parable, Jesus speaks of God as having unlimited patience; God is forgiving, one who is willing to let us grow before making judgments about us. That patient quality of God's is a wonderful thing since we can go through so many changes in our lives. I wonder how many of those people stacking sand bags together had malice in their hearts towards others a few weeks before. But now they are unified for the common good. People often change, and change for the better. And it's nice to have a God who knows that, one who has patience to give us the benefit of the doubt, one who waits and sees before he makes any final judgments.

There was an interesting movie by John Carpenter a few years back called *Escape from New York* in which the government walled off the entire city and put every criminal in the United States there where they could roam freely and do whatever they wanted, provided that they didn't threaten the perfect society outside the walls. The only problem with that concept is that there is good and bad in each one of us. To have a perfect society, you'd have to cram everybody in the world into New York City and there would be nobody left outside the walls to enjoy the purity.

God would just as soon let the good and the bad grow together throughout the world and make the best of an ugly situation. Maybe the good could even save the bad and turn the ugly into beauty.

A teacher once had two Freds in her class at opposite poles of the behavioral scale. Fred number one was well-disciplined, attentive, interested, highly motivated, courteous, and considerate. Fred number two, on the other hand, was rude, disruptive, lazy, late, sassy, bored, and uncooperative. One night at the parent-teacher conferences, a polite lady entered the classroom and introduced herself as Fred's mother. Assuming that she was the mother of Fred number one, the teacher lavishly praised him, saying that he was a fine boy and a real joy to have in her class.

The following morning, Fred came dashing into the classroom before the other students, and threw his arms around his teacher. "Thank you," he half sobbed, "for telling my mother that I was one of your favorite students, and a joy to have in class!" It turned out to be Fred number two. He said, "I know I haven't been very good, but I will be from now on!" Eventually, he did become one of her favorite students and was a joy to have in her classroom.

That story may be a bit contrived and unreal. But, if we all had the forgiveness and the patience of God in our hearts like the teacher did, little seeds of kindness and love carefully planted by each one of us could make this world a paradise. This world could become a

true kingdom of God where we could peacefully live and grow together in spite of all our faults.

Delivered at the Church of St. John in Grand Marais
on the Sixteenth Sunday of the Church Year
July 18, 1993

Pilgrims on Parade

The prophet Elijah made an incredible journey of over twenty miles through the desert to experience God's presence on Mount Sinai in a gentle breeze. St. Peter made an incredible journey of a few footsteps on top of the water to experience God's presence in the gentle but firm handshake of his best friend, Jesus Christ.

For Elijah the modest encounter with God was enough to rejuvenate his worn-out life and give him the strength and courage he needed to go on with the unpopular task of being a prophet of God. For St. Peter, it was enough to dispel his fear and to rekindle his faith so that he could be one of Christ's most ardent disciples.

It seems that if we put some effort into our spiritual lives, we are often rewarded with special little experiences of God's love which tend to elevate our existence to a higher level and give us the added spiritual strength we need to help us survive as Christians in an often hostile environment.

One of the traditional ways to put forth that effort is to make a pilgrimage, a special journey to an out-of-the-way place where we expect to meet God face to face. Such spiritual treks are just as effective in today's world as they were three thousand years ago in Elijah's day and age.

I made the same journey to Mount Sinai when I visited Israel for five months as a seminarian. We started out at the base of the mountain at about two o'clock in the morning, and arrived at the top just as the sun was rising over the other peaks. It made a spectacular red glow in the sky. It was a great experience of God's presence, and it was there in a prayer that I made a final decision to become a priest.

Three years ago, Larry Scully and I journeyed to the province of Quebec on a little pilgrimage. We visited Notre Dame Cathedral in Montreal, the Church of the Cap de Madeleine dedicated to Mary on the banks of the St. Lawrence River, and the Cathedral of St. Anne de Beaupre, dedicated to Mary's mother, a few miles up the shore from the city of Quebec. That journey seemed to charge me with spiritual energy. Looking back on my life, it was that pilgrimage which gave me the courage to live with my cancer.

Last year, I had the blessed opportunity to visit the sacred shrine of Lourdes in France. It was a great pilgrimage. It's impossible to describe what it's like to be among a crowd of thousands of other pilgrims, each person traveling thousands of miles to be at exactly the same spot to meet Christ in a special way, and each person filled with expectation, hope, and faith. And yet we were all part of the same body of believers, all in tune with every pilgrim who has ever been or will ever be there. With such company it's hard not to have an incredible experience of God's presence. It was there that I rediscovered how much God, Jesus, and Mary love me. It's like Jesus extended his hand to me in a saving gesture of love and gave me the spiritual strength I needed to accept and to live with my physical condition. I knew then that no amount of discomfort or disease would ever separate me from the love of God.

Well, this weekend, we have twenty-some parishioners, young and old, taking off on a pilgrimage to see the Pope in Denver, Colorado. We are excited about the chance to have a spiritual experience whose memory will hopefully last a lifetime. There may be so many people there that we may not even get to see the Pope unless we bring a telescope. But that shouldn't matter too much because we're all part of one body of Christ and the people at the front of the crowd will be our eyes.

Did I tell you about the time I saw the Pope in Rome? It was on the same seminarian trip to the Holy Land where I climbed Mount Sinai. I was standing at the head of the crowd in St. Peter's Square dressed in my clergy suit and Roman collar. The pope-mobile stopped near me, and the Pope got out. I thought to myself, "Boy, he's coming over to give me a special priest's blessing!" But he walked right by me and went over to a tramp dressed in rags with a filthy duffel bag at his feet. The Pope made a big sign of the cross over him, and returned to the vehicle.

Wanting the same for myself, I paid the tramp fifty bucks for his clothes and duffel bag, and came out the next week expecting a blessing. The Pope came by again and stopped right next to me. He came up to me and said: "I thought I told you to pick this garbage up and get it out of here!"

That story is obviously a fabrication. But I did get to see the Pope in St. Peter's Square, and the impact he had on the thousands of people who came to see him was incredible. It was like you could feel the Holy Spirit move across the crowd and inspire everyone there. As one of the Gospel writers once observed in Galilee, "The rejoicing in that vicinity rose to a fever pitch!"

While we are on pilgrimage, you can be on pilgrimage as well. Take a little trip to your favorite holy spot every day, light your candle if you have one, and spend five minutes of quiet time in God's presence. As you are praying for the success of our journey, we will be praying for you as well, especially if you leave your prayer request in the box at the back of the church after Mass today.

Delivered at the Church of St. John in Grand Marais
on the Nineteenth Sunday of the Church Year
August 7, 1993

More Urgent Than Usual

*An incomparable destiny awaits
those who have honored their Christian vocation.*

Paul VI

More Urgent Than Usual

The longer we live, the closer we all get to our deaths. I guess my situation isn't really much different from anybody else's, it's just a little more immanent to me. Consequently, today's Gospel also seems to be a little more urgent to me than usual.

I was reflecting on things I'd like to have carved on my tombstone. One idea that popped into my mind was the phrase, "He died a virgin." I'm kind of proud of that. It's not an easy thing in today's world to remain a virgin. But it's amazing what you can give up when you have your eyes focused on something infinitely better—like the kingdom of God, for example!

That's what today's gospel parable is all about—setting our priorities. What are we willing to sacrifice in order to live fully in God's presence? Ultimately, we have to give up everything through death to achieve everlasting life in his kingdom. But how about now in this present life? What are we willing to surrender to be near Christ right now?

In the first reading we are introduced to young King Solomon. God offers him anything his heart desires. However, Solomon is willing to give up all the riches of the world just to be a wise king. God praises his priorities. Solomon truly has his heart set on the kingdom and sacrifices everything else to go after it.

The first apostles offer a similar inspiring example as they left their fishing nets, families, friends, and the security of their home life. They gave up everything they had just to follow a homeless, itinerant preacher. They saw in his eyes and his words and his actions a loving, caring person who would transform the world into God's kingdom of light, happiness, and peace. And they wanted to be part of that no matter what the cost. That kingdom was worth more to them than all personal possessions.

The same thing happens in our day, too. We have the example of Linda Delonais who is giving up her old way of life to think about joining a religious order as a nun. I think it's very exciting to see someone in our midst living out today's Gospel the way she is.

Matthew is writing his Gospel to a community of Jews who became early Christians. They, too, had to give up their former friends, society, and traditions. It was tough on them, a huge sacrifice. In response to Jesus, they had to leave father and mother, pick up their crosses, and follow him! The kingdom didn't always seem that close to them. They often wondered why they gave up the old way for this new life. They may have reflected on the slaves of Egypt getting their freedom and then finding themselves lost in the Sinai desert for forty years.

But we, too, can have that same confidence that Christ knows. A lot of times we feel unappreciated for the anonymous little things we sacrifice to help his kingdom grow. But Christ knows, cares, and appreciates it immensely.

I want to change tacks slightly to tell you about one of my favorite saints, St. Ignatius of Antioch. He was a martyr, killed in the arena in Rome in the second century. He was like St. Paul in that he was constantly writing letters to various Christian communities throughout the Mediterranean. As he was being carted off to Rome to be tortured, the people decided to do some letter writing of their own, pleading with the Roman authorities to let St. Ignatius go free. He wrote a famous response in one of his later letters:

> Do not intercede on my behalf. Let me be ground to death by the teeth of lions to form a perfect loaf of bread for Christ. In this way I shall get to God. If the Lord's passion is a sham, so is my being in chains! As it is, however, I have given myself up completely to death, fire, sword, and wild beasts for the simple reason that near the sword means near to God. To be with wild beasts means to be with God. But, it must all be in the name of Jesus Christ. To share in his passion, I go through everything. For he who became the perfect man gives me the strength. Come fire, cross, battling with wild beasts, wrenching of bones, mangling of limbs, crushing of my whole body, cruel tortures of any kind—only let me get to God. If suffer I must, I shall be emancipated by Jesus Christ; and, united to him, I shall rise to freedom!

Those are great words, spoken by a man who backed them up by his inspiring example. They provide much reassurance to people like me who have terminal diseases. Since there is no way we can change our physical conditions anyway, why not accept them and embrace them, and use them as positive experiences to grow closer to Christ spiritually?

In that context today's gospel takes on rich meaning. I have begun to become less attached to this world and the things in it. The Twins' win-loss record seems to have less influence on my happiness. The persistent bad news coming out of Vikings' training camp seems to bother me less than in other years. My video library of movies and my collection of classical music albums seems unimportant. There's no way I can take them out of this world with me. So I have over six hundred tapes in my living room waiting to be taken by anybody who wants them. Feel free to come in and take your favorite movies. I have my heart set on a greater spiritual gift and none of these physical objects is going to get in my way.

Life on earth is a great gift from God, but a passing one to be sure. Let us set our hearts on the greater gifts to be shared with Christ forever in a new life somewhere else.

Delivered at the Church of St. John in Grand Marais
on the Seventeenth Sunday of the Church Year
August 24, 1993

Suffering Is Essential for Human Growth

We are introduced to the character of Job in the first reading today. He doesn't sound like the type of guy you would try to spend a pleasant afternoon with. He is constantly complaining about his miserable life and cursing the day he was born. But if anyone has a right to complain, I guess Job does.

What is missing from today's reading is the description of the many great tragedies that have befallen Job. The Book of Job starts when Job is a good man, special and pleasing in the eyes of God. He is wealthy and has a big family, all of whom are healthy. Then all of a sudden terrible things begin to happen. Job's farm was burned, his animals were destroyed, his servants were killed, and his ten children all died when the roof collapsed on them. To top it all off, Job himself was struck down with leprosy.

So in today's reading we find Job questioning the misery and suffering in his life. Why God? What is the sense of it? If you are a loving and caring God, how can you permit suffering and death to go on in the world.

You've heard the story of George? He is a good man with a fine family, all of whom practice Christian values. He is involved in a one-car accident. He asks, "Why me, God?"

Later, skiing, he breaks his back and lies in the hospital in a body cast. He asks again, "Why me, God?"

Later, he attempts to enter church one Sunday in a wheelchair but tumbles head first into a snow bank. Again, he asks, "Why me, God?"

A voice from heaven answers, "You know, George, there's something about you that I just don't like."

This is just a story, of course. The God we know is not the one I just pictured. God does not play with people's lives. He does not inflict suffering and punishment for our sins. We can all look at people in our lives, and it's immediately apparent that suffering is more a matter of chance than of divine judgment. The good suffer as much as the bad.

133

I think a big misconception that a lot of people have is that the suffering that comes to us is God's will, or that we somehow deserve it. Many of us have the impression that God is a great puppet master who pulls our strings, controls our lives, and determines what will happen to us, and when. God is not a chess master and we are not his pawns. God has made us free people with our individual human dignity. Because he has allowed us our own freedom, much of what happens to us in life is a matter of chance. Suffering, too, can be more a matter of chance than divine judgment. The fact that we must endure suffering in life does not mean that God does not love us or care about us.

Jesus, too, suffered. He suffered more than some of us ever will. He, too, died. Yet he was God's beloved son. So it's easy to see that God loves us. Suffering does not mean God does not care for us. In fact, this is where today's gospel comes in.

Jesus is on the scene healing and curing people to show us that God does care for us. Through miracles like these, he gives us faith and hope for the future. God does have power over life and death and some day we will be free of human suffering.

You might ask, "Why doesn't God work miracles all the time? Why must I continue to suffer my mental and physical agonies? Why can't my loved one be cured of disease?" That would be the easy way out. Suffering is essential for human growth. Without it, we become like spoiled, little children. Even when Christ was dying on the cross, people were saying, "You have the power; why don't you save yourself?" Jesus refused to give in to this human weakness.

Jesus' message to us in his refusal to perform a miracle for himself is that suffering is the way to glory. Through death comes life. When we suffer in this life, we share in Christ's passion. We can be certain that we will also share in his glory. If Christ were to work miracles in our lives every time a difficulty came along, we would be weak, limp shells with nothing inside. Our lives would be meaningless. By enduring the sufferings that come our way, we grow in our understanding of Christ and his love for us.

There is a great scene in the movie *The Robe* in which Richard Burton meets a paralyzed woman on a stretcher. He claims that Jesus is a fake because he could not cure her. This reminds me that there are three spiritual ways for us to deal with our sufferings: first, like Job, we can curse, complain, say how unfair life is, blame God for our misfortunes, and give up our faith out of anger and bitterness;

second, we can try and take the easy way out, as did the crowds in today's gospel, and run after Jesus demanding miracles, in which case we would have to demand more and more miracles because we would never learn how to deal with suffering; or third, we can be like that inspiring paralyzed woman in *The Robe* and learn to accept our suffering. We can learn to accept God as a loving, caring God in spite of our suffering. God knows that we suffer. God willingly took on human flesh to share in our suffering.

Rather than being the cause of our suffering, God is the one who can give us strength to cope with it. Now we must turn to him in faith and prayer. Just as he did with Peter's mother, Jesus will take our hand in his and comfort us in our afflictions as we pass with him from suffering and death into resurrection.

Delivered at the Church of St. John in Grand Marais
Undated

Songs of Farewell

Reading today's gospel makes me wonder what my future holds in store for me. Only God knows for sure, and he's not telling. I plan to get some chemotherapy and see what happens next. Maybe I'll get better, or maybe I'll get weaker and fade away into oblivion.

Three things I do know for sure: first, I know that I am too weak right now to continue working as a pastor; second, I know that I am ready to accept whatever comes my way; and third, I know that if the worst scenario occurs, I have today's gospel to fall back on—the joy of having a chance to share in Christ's passion and death, and the hope that I will also share in his resurrection.

So I'm going to take a few months off and see how things go. I love you all and will miss you very much.

Today, I thought I'd sing you my swan song, then play for you my favorite vocalist, and then let my favorite composer melt your heart with a final piece.

For my part, I'll sing "Four Strong Winds," by Judy Collins, with a few changes in the words:

> Four strong winds that blow lonely,
> seven seas that run high,
> all those things that don't change, come what may!
> for the good times, they are gone,
> and I'm bound for movin' on.
> I'll look for you if I'm ever back this way.
>
> Think I'll head out to Quebec;
> the trees are nice there in the fall.
> I've got some shrines that I can go and pray before,
> and I know that God will stay at my side
> through every day,
> and he'll guard me from all harm forever more.
>
> [harmonica]
>
> When winter gets long and dark,
> and the winds blow chilly and cold,

I will warm my heart with thoughts of each of you,
and the memories that we've shared
    will remind me how you cared,
and that will be enough to see me through!

Four strong winds that blow lonely,
seven seas that run high,
all those things that don't change, come what may,
for the good times are all gone,
and I'm bound for movin' on.
I'll look for you if I'm ever back this way!

For you are beautiful, and I have loved you dearly,
more dearly than the spoken word can tell.

For the second piece, I have a song on tape by Judy Collins that I'd like to play for you on the stereo. Judy Collins has always been my favorite female singer. Well, actually, my favorite singer was a girl friend at summer camp who used to serenade me with Judy Collins songs. The one she really melted my heart with is called "Who Knows Where the Time Goes." It expresses the mixture of sentiments that I have as I leave you today.

And finally, I'm going to end by calling on my old friend, Anton Bruckner, who was not only a mystical composer, but also a spiritual giant of the Catholic faith. We should all be proud to have him as part of our Catholic heritage. I always feel that playing his music in church is a great way to praise God. Usually, I play a piece of music that ends in glorious triumph. But today, I want to play a less dramatic piece that fades away into oblivion at the end, which may well be my fate as I said earlier.

This is Bruckner's song of farewell from the final six minutes of the third movement of his eighth symphony. The eighth symphony is an ingenious work of art that lasts eighty minutes and every bit of music in the entire symphony is based on a single seven-note theme. The part I will play starts off with a glorious crescendo based on an inversion of the main theme that builds to an exciting climax and is followed by a delayed cymbal clash. Just pretend that this part represents some of the great moments we've shared together here at St. John's. Then the music dies down with some lovely harp music as it turns morose for a minute or so; this section is reminiscent of the long, dark winters we have to endure on the North Shore. And finally, the piece ends with the most ingenious use of the main theme in which Bruckner takes the last four notes of the main theme and shifts them from a minor key to a glorious, sunshiny major key; in so doing he creates what I think are three minutes of the most beautiful, sublime music ever written. You'll know it when you hear the clarinet come in.

Bruckner's song of farewell represents for me the mixture of sadness at having to say good-bye, and the nostalgic joy of knowing that I take with me some wonderful memories of each one of you.

The final homily delivered at the Church of St. John in Grand Marais on the 22nd Sunday of the Church Year
August 29, 1993

Afterword

I heard a voice from heaven say to me:
"Write this down: Happy now are the dead
who die in the Lord!"
The Spirit added,
"Yes they shall find rest from all their labors,
for their good works accompany them."

Revelation 14:13

Obituary

Fr. Mark T. Hollenhorst of Grand Marais, Minnesota, died December 27, 1993, at his parents' home on Pelican Lake, near Brainerd, Minnesota, after an eight-year battle with medullary thyroid carcinoma. He was forty-three years old.

He was born May 2, 1950, in Rochester, Minnesota, to Dr. Robert W. and Alice Nolan Hollenhorst. His maternal grandparents were James J. and Nora T. Nolan of Brainerd. He graduated from Rochester Mayo High School in 1968, received a bachelor's degree from St. John's University, Collegeville, Minnesota, in 1974, and a master's in theology, also from St. John's, in 1977. He was ordained to the diaconate in 1976 and ordained as a priest in 1977 at St. John's Church in Rochester, Minnesota.

He served as a deacon at St. Francis Catholic Church in Brainerd in 1976–1977. After his ordination, he returned to St. Francis to serve as assistant pastor from 1977 to 1980. He was assistant pastor at Resurrection Church in Eveleth in 1980 to 1981 and from 1981 to 1985 at Blessed Sacrament Church in Hibbing. From 1985 to September 1993 he served as pastor of St. John's Catholic Church in Grand Marais and Holy Rosary Catholic Church in Grand Portage. He resigned from his duties in Grand Marais and Grand Portage on August 31 of that same year.

Mark devoted his life to helping others, especially youth and the homeless, through his work as a priest and through organizations such as the YMCA and the Boy Scouts. He also aided in the relocation of political refugees, and was an active member of the Lion's Club in Grand Marais. In the summer of 1993 he led a youth group to see Pope John Paul II in Denver. His hobbies included traveling, bridge, classical music, and collecting movies.

Survivors include his parents, two sisters and six brothers: Dr. Robert W., Jr., Duluth, Minnesota, Michael, Brainerd, Minnesota, Mary Lazarus, Millbrae, California, John, Salt Lake City, Utah, James, Saratoga, California, Kathleen Stassen, Sioux Falls, South

Dakota, Thomas, Alexandria, Virginia, and Stephen, Roseville, Minnesota, and twenty nieces and nephews.

Visitation and a wake service were at Holy Rosary Cathedral in Duluth, with funeral services also there on December 29, with Bishop Roger L. Schwietz presiding. A prayer service was then held in Grand Marais at St. John's Church with interment following in the St. John's cemetery.

Letter of Robert W. Hollenhorst, Sr., M.D.

Robert W. Hollenhorst, Sr., M.D.
Pequot Lakes, Minnesota
January 1, 1994

Dear Friends of Fr. Mark Hollenhorst:

We do appreciate your cards, letters, and memorials since our son died on December 27. His last two days of life were mostly spent in a semi or intermittent coma in which he experienced occasional frustration and little pain. There were long periods during which he spoke in rambling phrases or sentences, the content of which seemed to include a review of remembrances from the past, but none that were unpleasant or distressing to him. Sometimes he spoke with lucidity. He died peacefully holding my hand at twenty-six minutes after midnight, and believing fully in his union with God in heaven.

The religious services for Mark were very beautiful. On Tuesday, December 28, his Excellency, Roger Schwietz, Bishop of the Diocese of Duluth, conducted a vigil of prayer at five P.M. in the Cathedral of Our Lady of the Rosary in Duluth. On Wednesday at 9:30 A.M., Bishop Schwietz celebrated the funeral mass in the Cathedral. About fifty priests were present, and the church was filled with residents of the North Shore, from Two Harbors to Thunder Bay, from Duluth, Hibbing, Eveleth, Grand Marais, and Grand Portage; his brothers and sisters, their families, and other relatives and friends were also present. After a luncheon in the Holy Rosary School, family members traveled to Grand Marais where Fr. Mark Makowski, pastor of St. John's Church, conducted the Rites of Committal of the body of Fr. Mark Hollenhorst. Following this service, the body was buried in St. John's Catholic cemetery on the shore of Lake Superior at Grand Marais.

Sincerely,

Robert W. Hollenhorst, Sr., M.D.

Funeral Mass Homily

Homily delivered by Msgr. Bernard Popesh
at the Funeral Mass for Fr. Mark Hollenhorst
in the Cathedral of Our Lady of the Rosary
in Duluth, Minnesota
December 29, 1993

Fr. Mark Hollenhorst is now enjoying an eternal Christmas. His mother told me that he seemed to be waiting for Christmas before he died. On Christmas morning, he said, "December 25—Christmas," and he never went to sleep again until he died just after midnight on December 27.

As a theologian, and Father Mark was a good one, he knew that Christmas is described as a wonderful exchange:

God in love beyond imagining
comes down to be one with us;
So we through our love
can go up to be one with God.

And Father Mark must have been very aware that he was completing that wonderful exchange this Christmas.

That was so typical of the many blessings that God showered on Father Mark. When we look back on his life—as the first reading today mentioned—we won't think of the few years he had with us, but of the many beautiful experiences we had with him that really constituted the "fullness of life" mentioned in that reading.

In fact, I found it easy to know what to say on this occasion, for several reasons.

Sometimes we hear the remark that there are no characters among the priesthood today as there were in the past. Father Mark proves them wrong. The many stories about Father Mark like going to Mexico by way of Canada, playing his mouth organ and singing an original song as his farewell homily at St. Francis in Brainerd, or having one thousand videos, all carefully catalogued and classified, but not a single picture or hanging on his walls make him a legend as colorful as any characters of the past.

What is interesting to note today is that Father Mark had bought a grave site for himself in the cemetery at Grand Marais shortly after he was assigned there, before he had any hint of his sickness. And this was just his first assignment as a pastor!

We can never underestimate Father Mark. He had a great mind and a creative imagination with wide interests. How many would travel to Montana just to see an eclipse of the sun? How many would take a trip to Germany and Austria to visit where Gustave Mahler and Anton Bruckner, his favorite two composers, were born, worked, and died? (I learned that when he came to Bruckner's grave, he lay flat on it and whistled some of Bruckner's tunes, much to the bewilderment of the passersby.) How many could beat Father Mark in a game of bridge? He was indeed a character—a delightful character!

For another reason, I found it easy to know what to say here today. I knew that whatever I would say Father Mark would be up in heaven, remarking "That's the best homily I ever heard." Father Mark was the ultimate optimist—always speaking in superlatives. I admired him for never saying anything bad about anyone and, even more so, for never allowing anybody else to do so in his presence. That was a quality he attributed to the training he received from his mother.

We can attribute a lot more of the strong faith he had to his parents and family. And now, on behalf of the diocese, we wish to express our gratitude to them for giving us Father Mark, and our deepest sympathy for their loss: to his devoted parents, Robert and Alice, his sisters Mary and Kathleen, and his six brothers (a regular litany of the saints) Robert, Michael, John, James, Thomas, and Stephen.

We also should express our gratitude and sympathy to his other family, the parishioners of St. John's in Grand Marais and Holy Rosary in Grand Portage, who not only admired him as Father but adopted him as a son in their solicitude for him, especially during his illness.

Father Mark seemed to draw forth love by the love he offered. He was a genuine person, fully alive, always seeking the extraordinary, as the bishop mentioned at the wake last night, who just naturally exuded Christianity in his actions.

One can't fake it with young people. And young people as well as adults loved Mark wherever he was, as an assistant at Brainerd, Eveleth, and Hibbing, as pastor at Grand Marais and Grand Portage, and as chaplain to the Boy Scouts and as Spiritual Director of Teens Encounter Christ (TEC). And yet one always knew that Mark was the priest.

Finally, I found it easy to know what to say on this occasion because Father Mark's faith taught us how our faith can help us die. At the past clergy conference in October, Father Mark was honored for being the outstanding priest of the diocese this year. That honor was well deserved because of the inspiration he gave us, in the way he accepted his own death. His homilies, his articles in the newspapers, his appearance in the pro-life videos this year, and his private conversations have enriched the faith of us all.

Ordinarily, the death of a young priest, especially one that follows a prolonged illness, is considered a tragedy and is accompanied by much sorrow for the priest.

Not so with Mark's death. He got us all to accept it while he was still alive; and God cooperated with him by having it take place in the middle of this joyous season. In one of his homilies, he said, "It appears that my cancer is the way through which I will get to God." And in another, he remarked, "After my death, he will raise me up on the last day so that I can experience a total Easter of eternal joy." In that spirit and in keeping with his wishes—despite our own sorrow of losing him—let us make this a celebration of the great blessings of the resurrection that came to Father Mark Hollenhorst at this Christmas time.